CORPORATE VALUATION

THE WILEY/RONALD-NATIONAL ASSOCIATION OF ACCOUNTANTS PROFESSIONAL BOOK SERIES

CORPORATE VALUATION

A Business and Professional Guide

Gordon V. Smith

President
Associated Valuation Technologies, Inc.

WILEY

JOHN WILEY & SONS

New York • Chichester • Brisbane • Toronto • Singapore

Library of Congress Cataloging in Publication Data:

Smith, Gordon V., 1937–
  Corporate valuation.

  (Wiley/Ronald-National Association of Accountants
professional book series)
  Bibliography: p.
  1. Business enterprises—Valuation. I. Title.
II. Series.
HG4028.V3S58   1988   658.1'522   87-23114
ISBN 0-471-85826-9

Printed in the United States of America

10 9 8 7 6 5 4 3 2 1

TO *my illustrious colleagues*
with whom I learned this
profession,

TO *the demanding clients that*
urged us to develop it,

AND TO *Nancy, Craig, and Tracy*
who kept the home fires burning
while I was off doing both.

PREFACE

This book is for managers in business and government, accountants, attorneys, and other professionals. It has two primary objectives.

First, I would like to advance the image of appraisers as recognized professionals. I often refer to "professional appraisers" or "the appraisal profession." This comes naturally to me because I have viewed my career as a profession and because my associates through the years have exemplified that status. I must concede that, however, the general public does not recognize appraisers as professionals. Contrary to popular opinion, most appraisers did not learn their skills guessing people's weight on the boardwalk at Atlantic City.

I hope that this book will present appraising as the demanding, investigative analytic work that it is and provide an image of appraisers as the ethical, well-trained, and intelligent professionals that they are.

Second, I offer what I hope to be practical and useful guidance to those who may have the occasion to utilize valuations in business. In my experience, working with a knowledgeable client nearly always produces an appraisal of higher quality and at less cost than otherwise. With this book I hope to increase the numbers of such prospective clients for my colleagues and myself by providing:

1. Some standards by which to evaluate appraisers and appraisals.
2. Some guidance on how to seek out appraisal professionals who have the appropriate experience and background for a specific appraisal assignment.

3. Suggestions on how to work with an appraisal professional to maximize effectiveness and minimize cost.

4. A knowledge of the business situations that require an appraisal.

5. An understanding of how appraisals are made.

6. An introduction to accepted valuation methodologies.

7. An understanding of how appraisers work and the techniques they have available for different types of assets and assignments.

My intention is to accomplish these objectives by discussing these topics from the appraiser's point of view, not to make the reader an expert appraiser, but to provide an understanding of *what* appraisers do, *why* they do it, and *how* they do it.

GORDON V. SMITH

Moorestown, New Jersey
December 1987

ACKNOWLEDGMENTS

I would like to acknowledge the valuable assistance of my brother David, who helped to undangle the participles and reunite the infinitives in the manuscript; my colleagues John Goodman, Russell Parr, and Charles Jerominski, who constructively criticized some of the technical sections; my associates Dave Weiler, Larry Shanda, Vince Stolowski, Glenda Schrayer, and Betty Kraft, with whom I discussed these ideas; and my partner, Joe Brennan, who introduced me to the crazy entrepreneurial life that made it possible to do in the first place.

Figures are reprinted by permission of Associated Valuation Technologies, Inc., Moorestown, New Jersey.

Quotations and Figure 8.1 from *Engineering Valuation and Depreciation*, by Anson Marston, Robley Winfrey, and Jean Hempsted (© 1953; Iowa State University Press, 2121 South State Avenue, Ames, Iowa 50010), are reprinted by permission.

Quotations from Financial Accounting Standards Board, High Ridge Park, Stamford, Connecticut 06905, are reprinted with permission of the copyright holder. The complete document is available from the FASB.

CONTENTS

1

APPRAISERS AND APPRAISING

In the most generic sense, an appraisal is an opinion about the attributes of something. After a Presidential news conference we are accustomed to hearing television network news people *appraise* the questions and answers. One often hears the phrase," . . . an *appraisal* of the situation . . . ." Something can be *appraised* as to attractiveness, quality, style, size, weight, or color.

The concern here is with a specific form of appraisal, defined as a *written opinion of the monetary value of property*. Some colleagues will no doubt believe this an oversimplification, but the focus here is not on appraisers, but on clients and prospective clients and their need for a practical understanding of what appraisers do.

The chapters that follow analyze and provide examples of what constitutes a *written* opinion and how that *opinion* is developed. Also reviewed are the many permutations of *value* and the various meanings of *property*. The terms "valuation" and "appraisal" will be used interchangeably.

THE APPRAISER

An appraiser is the source of such an opinion of value. A professional appraisal is an estimate of value based upon investigations and analyses which are guided by well-defined principles and from which, to the greatest extent possible, personal bias has been removed. The appraiser, therefore, must have education, experience, and training that can provide the basis for this reasoned opinion.

An appraiser also has an obligation to assist a client in determining the correct type of value and level of precision to be achieved in a given assignment, so as to ensure, as far as possible, that the appraisal conclusion will meet client requirements and that its cost is commensurate with those requirements.

Form of Practice

A look at the Yellow Pages for any metropolitan area will reveal a substantial list of individual appraisers and appraisal firms. This might include:

1. *Individuals* practicing as sole proprietors or with temporary or part-time help.
2. *Small independent firms* with several employees and support staff, performing only appraisal work.
3. *Small combination firms* with several employees and support staff, performing appraisal work as an adjunct to some other activity, such as real estate or machinery brokerage, running auctions, or other consulting.
4. *Large independent firms* with perhaps several hundred employees and a national or international practice.
5. *Large combination firms*, as above, but operated as an adjunct to another primary line of business, such as an accounting practice, consulting, or banking.

In addition, many appraisers are either not listed in a directory or do not appear under the "Appraisers" heading. The *only requirement* to satisfy before presenting oneself to the public as an appraiser is the cost of stationery and business cards and perhaps some advertising. Many would-be appraisers move into this line of work on a part-time basis or as a "moonlighter" during those periods when appraisal work is in great demand (e.g., when falling interest rates produce a rash of property refinancings).

Retaining an appraiser is, then, a classic *caveat emptor* situation. Since no licensing or certification is required for appraisers by local, state, or federal government, buyers of appraisal services may feel left entirely on their own in the matter of selection. This situation is not so bleak as it may sound, as there are a number of reliable standards by which appraisers and appraisal firms can be judged. The following sections highlight these standards.

Professional Societies

Professional appraisers may belong to a number of organizations. These societies provide members an opportunity to interact with colleagues and to exchange information about changes within the profession. Some of these societies provide their membership with the opportunity to stay up-to-date via continuing specialized education, and some even require it as a condition for continued certification. Requirements for membership vary. The Appendix presents additional information about the organizations identified briefly below:

American Society of Appraisers. Membership is multi-disciplinary, international (though primarily in the United States), and numbers 5,500 in 80 chapters. Entrants must demonstrate experience and pass qualifying examinations, and Senior Members, who may use the designation ASA, must pass a written examination in their discipline and recertify every five years. Disciplines include: Appraisal Administration, Appraisal Education, Business Valuation, Machinery and Equipment, Personal Property, Technical Valuation, and Public Utilities.

American Institute of Real Estate Appraisers (also known as the Appraisal Institute and affiliated with the National Association of Realtors®). Certified members, who have met the basic educational and experiencial requirements and have successfully completed extensive course work and examinations, use the designations MAI (Member, Appraisal Institute) and RM (Residential Member).

Society of Real Estate Appraisers. With 17,000 members, the Society of Real Estate Appraisers offers its membership educational programs and requires course work, successful examination completion, and other experiencial and educational requirements for designation as Senior Residential Appraiser (SRA), Senior Real Property Appraiser (SRPA), and Senior Real Estate Analyst (SREA).

The Canadian Institute of Chartered Business Valuators or *Institut Canadien des Experts en Evaluation d'Enterprises*. Formerly, The Canadian Association of Business Valuators, the name was changed in 1985. The 400 members and associates specialize in appraising business enter-

prises and capital stock. The 200 full members use the designation
CBV (Chartered Business Valuator), or EEE (Expert en Evaluation
d'Enterprise).

Appraisal Institute of Canada or *Institut Canadien des Evaluateurs*. Established in 1938, this is the national association of real estate appraisers.
Membership numbers 6,200, of which 2,000 are designated AACI (Accredited Appraiser Canadian Institute), 1,100 are designated CRA (Canadian Residential Appraiser), and 3,100 are Candidates.

When evaluating the qualifications of an appraiser with respect to membership in professional societies, attention should be paid to:

1. Entrance requirements that combine demonstrated experience with
    successful completion of specialized course work and/or examinations.
2. Requirements for continuing education, active participation in the
    organization, and periodic recertification.
3. Enforceable sanctions within the organization for actions related to
    unethical practices.

Ethics

Each of the professional organizations mentioned above has developed standards of ethical conduct to which its membership is expected to adhere.
Each also has sanctions that are applicable for violations of those standards.
Certain common considerations found in these standards of ethical conduct
mandate that:

1. The appraiser can have no interest in the subject property, including
    ownership or acting as agent for its sale or financing.
2. The appraiser should not suppress or minimize facts or data that
    might be detrimental to a client position.
3. An appraiser cannot serve more than one client in the same matter
    except with the full knowledge and consent of both parties.
4. Fees for appraisal services cannot be contingent on the outcome of a
    court proceeding, successful financing, or other action, or be based
    upon a percentage of concluded value.
5. An appraisal assignment is confidential.

6. An appraiser has a fiduciary responsibility to the client and to the public.

7. An appraisal report must reveal clearly when conditions essential to the conclusion have been assumed on a hypothetical basis or when only one part of a homogeneous property is reported upon ("fractional appraisal").

8. An appraisal report must reveal all contingent and limiting conditions.

9. An appraisal assignment should not be undertaken if the appraiser does not have proper background or qualifications for the work or cannot devote the proper time or resources to accomplish the assignment competently.

Other matters may not be specifically addressed in codes of ethical standards but should be considered appropriate business practice. When discussing an assignment with a potential client, an appraiser should reveal unusual knowledge about the subject property or involved third parties that may have come about because of previous assignments or business relationships. In a case involving litigation, as an example, an appraiser should reveal if the law firm that may be adversarial to the prospective client has been, or is, representing a previous client. If a prospective client is acquiring property from a former client or business associate, the appraiser should volunteer this fact. In many cases, these former relationships will have no effect on the appraiser's ability to render an unbiased opinion, but they should be disclosed. If an appraiser has confidential information (e.g., "insider information") about a particular property or business that would preclude assurance of complete objectivity, the assignment should be refused. Under no circumstances should an appraiser trade in the stock or bonds of a client company or of a company being appraised. Even though a small stockholding in a large, publicly traded corporation would not materially benefit from most appraisal activity, the hint of conflict of interest would be present and might render the appraiser unable to be credible as an expert witness.

An appraiser should decline an engagement if client expectations are clearly, in the appraiser's opinion, not attainable or if the prospective client requests that assumptions be made that are not reasonable. This is simply proper business practice. If a prospective client is convinced that a 1983 Volkswagen was worth at least $20,000 before a building fell on it or that a swamp in Minnesota is suitable for a gambling casino site, it is only good sense to decline the appraisal engagement.

Education

Only a few sources of specialized appraisal training are available. The oldest of these is within the Engineering Department at Iowa State University, Ames, Iowa, where valuation courses have been offered for a number of years. The American Institute of Real Estate Appraisers offers an extensive calendar of courses at university locations throughout the United States.

In recent years, under the sponsorship of the American Society of Appraisers, a Valuation Sciences Degree program is being offered at six institutions:

Dyke College (Cleveland, Ohio).

Hofstra University (Hempstead, New York).

The Lindenwood Colleges (St. Charles, Missouri).

Loretto Heights College (Denver, Colorado).

Skidmore College (Saratoga Springs, New York).

Southwest Texas State University (San Marcos, Texas).

The educational background of practicing professional appraisers therefore is extremely varied and will probably always be so, in spite of the growth of specialized training. This is due, in part, to the extremely varied requirements of the profession itself. There are really two levels of "education" required to become an appraiser. The first of these concerns the principles and techniques of valuation and is acquired either "on the job" or through the completion of specialized education. (See institutions listed above.) The second level relates to knowledge about specific types of property, industry segments, accounting, economics, taxation, and regulatory matters, that one can acquire in other educational programs or via general business experience. The development of good analytical and communications skills is essential.

An individual appraiser cannot and need not be expert in everything, any more than can an accountant, attorney, or banker, all of whom are called upon to apply their particular professional expertise in a variety of business situations. It does not require an electronics expert to appraise a patent on an electronic device any more than it does to account for its income, to support litigation on it, or to lend money on it. What *is* required is a thorough knowledge of appraisal methodology, the ability to communicate with those who *are* expert in the field, the ability to research the technology and its business prospects, to apply recognized appraisal principles, and finally to weigh the result with sound judgment.

Although appropriate educational background should be a consideration in evaluating an appraiser, one should not become too "hung up" on the presence or absence of specific education.

Specialization

Thirty years ago, professional appraisal practice was almost completely limited to real estate, machinery, gems and jewelry, and fine arts. Valuations of business enterprises or securities were uncommon and were often based on the values of underlying physical assets. The existence of intangible assets in a business was recognized as "goodwill" and attributed to the owner or the business location. Today, commerce has become more complex, service enterprises with few fixed assets have grown in size and number, and governmental regulations become ever more pervasive. The appraisal profession has changed as well. As are other professionals, appraisers are becoming increasingly specialized.

Appraisal specialties, or disciplines as they are often called, are mixed classifications with sometimes unclear boundaries. One way they can be logically arranged is by type of property, such as:

1. Real estate (land and improvements).
2. Machinery and equipment.
3. Fine arts.
4. Gems.
5. Antiques.
6. Securities.
7. Business enterprises.
8. Intangible property.

In other cases, appraisal disciplines are defined according to the purpose of the valuation, such as:

1. Insurance.
2. *Ad valorem* (property) taxation.
3. Condemnation.

4. Utility regulation.
5. Income taxation.
6. Litigation support.

Increasingly, appraisal assignments require the full- or part-time participation of appraisers from two or more disciplines in a team effort.

AN OVERVIEW OF THE APPRAISAL PROCESS

Any appraisal engagement, from the smallest to the largest, comprises several distinct tasks: (1) project definition and planning, (2) investigation, (3) analysis, and (4) reporting.

Project Definition and Planning

In order to maximize the results of these tasks, an appraisal engagement must be well defined and carefully planned. This is especially true of large engagements where there may be several appraisal disciplines involved, perhaps 30 to 40 appraisers, and multiple locations and business entities.

Project Definition.   This stage concerns the establishment of the essential facts and underlying assumptions that will be the principal specifications of the assignment and includes:

1. Identifying the client.
2. Defining the appraisal purpose.
3. Establishing the appraisal date ("as of" date).
4. Specifying the premise of value (definition of value required for the purpose).
5. Identifying property to be included.
6. Identifying property to be excluded.
7. Identifying property locations to be included.
8. Specifying the form and content of the report.
9. Agreeing upon delivery date(s).

These parameters define the task for the appraiser and the client, and, if carefully done and reviewed by both, will greatly assist in avoiding later misunderstanding.

One might well question why there is a need to establish the *purpose* of an appraisal before proceeding. Isn't there only one right value? Are there different values for different clients and different situations? This sounds like "different strokes for different folks" and smacks of dishonesty. As in many things, the answer is yes and no. Yes, there are different appraisal purposes that require different value definitions and valuation methods. For example, if you desire to know the value of your automobile *for sale to a dealer*, its value is best measured by retail selling prices, reduced by the dealer's holding costs and profit. If you desire to sell your automobile yourself on the open market, the best measure of value would be the unadjusted retail selling prices of similar models in comparable condition. Two values and two appraisal methods are valid for two different purposes.

In another situation, the value of closely held (not traded on an exchange) common stock to establish estate tax liability is a uniqe value, and there are recognized methods for its estimation. That value should not change whether the client is the taxpayer or the Internal Revenue Service.

An appraisal of property for insurance placement or proof of loss is usually on the basis of cost of replacement less physical depreciation (some insurance policies differ) and should be the same for the insurer or the insured. Again, the purpose determines the type of value and appraisal methodology.

Later discussion will amplify these rules, which are highlighted here to illustrate the importance of carefully defining "to whom and for what purpose" an appraisal is to be made.

In a complex engagement, defining the property inclusions and exclusions, ownerships, and locations is not as easy as one might imagine. A large, international corporate entity may have hundreds of locations and legal business entities that do not coincide with operating business segments and divisions. All of this must be known to the appraiser so that the product of the appraisal work is meaningful to the client.

As an example, consider an appraisal assignment involving a manufacturing operation that, to any observer, appears to be a single, homogeneous plant. In actuality, the land and certain buildings are leased from the local government. The U.S. government owns some of the machinery. Other machinery is leased from third parties or from a partnership of company management, and some machinery is owned. All of this property may have to be appraised; but if it is not segregated properly in the work, the values of the individual ownerships cannot be later determined. Proper planning can prevent this situation and thereby the cost of its correction.

Planning.   This stage involves defining the logistics of accomplishing the valuation, including a determination of:

1.   Appraisal disciplines required.
2.   Professional staff time requirements of each.
3.   Delivery commitments and availability of property access.
4.   Minimization of travel and related living expenses.
5.   Allocation of resources to the various appraisal tasks.
6.   Information requirements from the client.
7.   Need for outside specialists.
8.   Organization of the project team.

In an engagement involving one or two appraisers and a single location or business entity, the planning stage may be simple and covered in a brief telephone conversation. In the most complex engagement, the project plan should be written, and may require a computerized project planner, with interim task deadlines, PERT charts, and the like.

Investigation

The amount of investigative activity can vary considerably. In some situations this task involves minimal work effort, such as when the appraiser's client does not have access to the property being valued or when the client does not wish any contact between the property owner (or employees) and the appraiser. This does not necessarily imply any impropriety, as there may be many valid reasons for these conditions. The appraiser will then work with the information available, making assumptions about data that are not accessible, and qualify the appraisal report accordingly.

   The more typical situation is where full access to the subject property is present. The investigation then proceeds in a number of steps.

Property Description.   Description can be relatively straightforward. For physical property a description would customarily include:

1. Land legal descriptions, survey, tax maps.
2. Building specifications, measurements, previous appraisals, photographs.
3. Machinery and equipment manufacturer, model, serial number, speed, size, options, motor(s).

However, when the appraisal concerns a business enterprise or capital stock, the property description will include consideration of:

1. Historical financial information.
2. Data relative to issues of stock and other securities, stockholders, and board of directors.
3. Sales and expense forecasts.
4. Capital requirements in the future.
5. History of the business.
6. Product line information.
7. Competition.
8. Suppliers, contracts.
9. Licenses, certifications, compliance.

When intangible assets are part of the appraisal investigation, the property description phase can be quite complex. In addition to the items noted above for a business enterprise, the description would include:

1. Employee rosters and salaries, training information.
2. Data on customers, sales methods, distributors.
3. Descriptions of computer software.
4. Copies of patents, trademarks, copyrights.
5. Descriptions of advertising programs, marketing studies, training materials.

Field Investigation. In nearly every appraisal situation some investigation at the property location is necessary. This can be a visit of several hours for the appraisal of a small business enterprise or hundreds of professional staff days of effort over several weeks for a full corporate property valuation.

From the items listed for the description phase, one can visualize that, in an appraisal of a large property that includes several asset classifications, the field investigation can be costly and time-consuming and can require the participation of many client personnel. The entire effort must be well organized in order to minimize disruption of the ongoing business. One organizational technique is to have a "kick-off" meeting with appropriate levels of management in order to review the appraisal purpose and the requirements for information. The kick-off accomplishes several things:

1. Each participant receives a consistent explanation of the background and objectives of the project.
2. Any questions that are raised which affect more than one party can be addressed for the benefit of all.
3. Each participant can better plan how to assemble the required information and staff personnel, so that when interviews are scheduled, they can proceed efficiently.
4. Clearances, confidentiality agreements, and letters of introduction can be arranged.
5. Scheduling can be discussed so that peak work periods, plant closings, business trips, trade shows, and conventions can be accommodated.

Analysis

In this phase, the appraiser addresses each of the identified assets to be included, determining the appropriate valuation methodology and performing the calculations of value. As explained in later chapters, this task may involve several iterations with respect to individual assets in order to achieve, in the appraiser's judgment, a logical balance of value conclusions. The results of analysis may cause the appraiser to return to the investigative task for additional information about the property, perhaps from external sources.

Typically, this work takes place away from the client location or the property and does not involve client personnel. When appraising physical assets, it is not uncommon for the analysis phase to require a work effort equal to the field investigation. For intangible assets or a business enterprise, the analysis may require three to four times the effort of the field investigation.

Reporting

In accord with the nature of the assignment or the wishes of the client, reporting may take several forms:

1. A verbal report of initial, unrefined conclusions.
2. A preliminary written report in outline form.
3. A draft of a final report with narrative and/or supporting schedules.
4. A final narrative report with exhibits, schedules, photographs.
5. Direct testimony in written or verbal form.

Chapter 10 presents a sample appraisal report and examines its essential parts.

2
SELECTING AND WORKING
WITH AN APPRAISER

The selection of a professional appraiser may be a "start-from-scratch" effort, beginning with a directory search or, in the case of a well-publicized corporate acquisition, a process of elimination applied to several firms seeking an opportunity to serve the acquiring corporation. Similarly, working with an appraiser may be as simple as defining the assignment or as extensive as providing extensive liaison in a team effort lasting several months.

THE SELECTION PROCESS

Searching

As noted earlier, the Yellow Pages are replete with appraisers and appraisal firms. This is not to suggest, however, that the Yellow Pages are the best source of valuation counsel. As when moving to a new community and seeking a doctor or dentist, consulting directories of professional societies or requesting referrals are two well-used techniques.

Some well-known professional societies of appraisers were noted earlier. If they do not have a local telephone listing, a call to their national headquarters will produce a contact in their local organization. If you explain your appraisal requirements as fully as possible, the names of individuals and firms will be forthcoming.

As for referrals, the idea is relatively easy, but the execution may be difficult. We once asked a former college roommate, who has become a physician, how, when moving to a new community, to discover a good dentist. His answer was that if we could locate any doctor with whom we were satisfied, ask that doctor for a referral, even if it was unrelated to his practice. The rationale is that professionals of approximately equal skill and reputation move in the same circles and are likely to know (and recommend) one another.

The same principle applies to other professionals, appraisers included. An accountant, attorney, or business associate (or competitor!) may be a source of these referrals.

Initial Screening

Obviously, the approaches will differ for an appraisal situation involving a single location or business as opposed to a national or multinational organization. The various appraisal disciplines already mentioned, and the extent to which a multi-disciplinary approach is necessary, are also considerations.

The nature of the problem should dictate the choice of valuation consultant. Do not retain a large, national firm to appraise an uncomplicated piece of real estate for possible sale. A qualified local appraiser is probably better equipped for this task, and can accomplish it more economically and probably more accurately. If the value of this property will become the focus of a hard-fought *ad valorem* tax litigation, the local appraiser may still be the best choice, but one should seek an individual or firm with strong credentials in this arena. If, on the other hand, the property is so large that it enters into the national market or is of such special purpose that it requires a broader base of experience, then a larger firm should be the choice.

One objective of this book is to provide an understanding of the guidelines in making such choices.

For a relatively straightforward assignment the initial screening can be done by telephone. Be prepared to provide the prospective firm with:

1. Location of the property.
2. Size of the property (i.e., acreage, square footage, number of machines, size of the business).
3. Type of business or product.
4. Your delivery requirements.
5. Purpose of the appraisal.

If you do not wish, in this initial interview, to divulge specific information about the property to be appraised, omit the identifying elements and understand that the appraiser's responses may also have to be somewhat imprecise.

Having provided this information, there are several questions that you should have answered:

1. Is this type of property within the firm's area of expertise?
2. Have they done similar work before?
3. For whom?
4. Can they meet the delivery requirement?
5. What is a broad range of fee?

What do the answers tell you? First, you will have an indication how the firm treats an inquiry. Do they sound professional? Do they return telephone calls? Do they seem indifferent? These things may seem very subjective, and they are, but an appraiser's "character" is very important, and this telephone interview may be your first glimpse of it.

Do not be put off if you do not receive a long list of former clients in a telephone conversation. Appraisal assignments are confidential and the appraiser can only discuss those assignments about which there is no sensitivity relative to an appraisal having been made. The appraiser may describe former assignments in terms of the size of client, type of business, or geographical area. The appraiser may not wish to quote a fee, or even a broad range of fees, over the phone. This is not critical at this stage. The main purpose of these questions is to get a "feel" for the firm's clientele and to determine whether they understand the assignment.

Request a capabilities brochure with personnel qualifications from those firms or individuals that give a favorable impression and who seem to have the proper expertise and can meet your delivery requirements. Indicate that you will contact them after reviewing this material. At the end of this procedure you should have several viable candidates.

Interviews

For an engagement of any size, several appraisal firms or individuals should be interviewed. This is especially important when one has little experience in appraisal matters or with appraisal professionals. Following the initial screening process, the next step is to meet the candidates face to face. We suggest two stages because some candidates will be eliminated in the first step or because the selection process may be completed there.

First-Stage Interview.   This interview should involve only you and one or two representatives of the candidate firm. The purpose is for them to provide additional information about the firm and their professional credentials and for you to provide whatever additional information about the assignment you feel comfortable in offering.

If in these first-stage interviews you feel confident enough to make the selection, you can engage the firm then and there. If you intend to go on with more extensive interviews, inform the candidates that they will be contacted for a formal presentation with other members of your management team.

Second-Stage Interview.   This stage involves a presentation to a small management team by the firms that appear to be the most qualified. By this time, the candidates have met you and received some information about the assignment. You, in turn, will have learned how the appraisers view the scope of the work and its specifications and also some idea of how they view the magnitude of the work in terms of fee. You can proceed with presentations on one of two bases:

1. That you let the candidates define the scope of work and the appraisal specifications and provide them data, upon request, to the extent that you can.
2. That you will provide a package of data to all candidates, together with some specifications that you have created.

You must consider the advantages and disadvantages of both approaches. When you give free rein to the candidates and merely state your appraisal problem to them and ask for their best solution:

1. You run the risk that the proposals you receive for the assignment will be so dissimilar that you cannot compare them, and a whole new round of negotiations will be necessary.
2. An otherwise superior firm may get "off track" and be eliminated from consideration because of lack of direction from you.

3. You get the benefit of the original thinking of each firm in their approach to the problem, and thereby provide yourself the opportunity for a more creative discussion in the presentation process.

When you approach the second-stage interview as more of a bidding process and provide each candidate with a "bid package" and specifications for the work:

1. You have more assurance that the proposals will be uniform, will address the same tasks, and will be therefore comparable.
2. You take some responsibility for the proposals (and fee quotes!), since you are setting the specifications.
3. You may stifle some original thinking in the candidates' effort to stay within the letter of the "bid package."

You may want to consider retaining an appraiser to assist in the development of information provided to candidates and in the selection process or in the writing of a "Request for Proposal." This could be an individual or firm that is not qualified to bid on the work because of size, possible conflict of interest, inability to meet delivery requirements, and so on.

Formal Presentation. Whichever course you decide upon, the next step is to notify the candidates that you are requesting a formal presentation. Several essential elements should be included in this request:

1. A definitive fee quote as part of the presentation.
2. A recitation of the firm's qualifications.
3. A description of the appraisal "team" and the qualifications of its principal members.
4. A projection of the assets the firm expects to find and how these will be appraised.
5. An appointment to meet the firm member who will be responsible for the engagement.
6. The schedule for the completion of the various appraisal tasks and how the progress will be monitored.

These elements are discussed below in more detail.

Client Briefing. You should provide a briefing at the outset of the formal presentation which would include:

1. A description of the events leading up to the appraisal need.
2. A description of the property to be included.
3. The reason for the appraisal, as you see it.
4. An introduction to the relevant personnel within your company and other outside professionals who may be involved.
5. Delivery requirements.

Review of Qualifications. The appraiser should provide information about the firm in general and individuals who may be assigned to the project.

Presentation of Methods. You should request, if the presentation does not include it, a discussion of valuation methodologies that may be employed by the appraiser, the data that may be required, and any special conditions that the appraiser may expect to encounter. The purpose of this is not to let you indicate your preference for methodology, but rather to permit your evaluation of the appraiser's competence.

Preview Conclusions. Resist the temptation to ask for value conclusions, unless you simply want to test the appraiser, who should not give "off-the-cuff" conclusions anyway.

References. It is perfectly correct to ask for references when you are truly in doubt about a firm's past performance. Appraisers do not want to burden previous clients and are understandably reluctant to provide references indiscriminately. Ask for references only if the firm is seriously being considered and if you have genuine concerns.

Project Management. You should expect a well-thought-out project plan, especially for large, multi-disciplinary engagements. This should include the tasks that would be performed and the schedule for each.

Delivery Requirements. From the project plan you should be able to satisfy yourself that sufficient resources are available to meet the delivery required.

Staffing. The project plan should include a recitation of the principal staff members that the firm expects to utilize on the project, together with their respective roles in the engagement.

Management Review. On a large engagement, there should be a provision for reviews of the work by the firm's top management or by a review team not involved in the project.

Many appraisal firms, as do other consulting organizations, employ sales representatives as a practical way to obtain adequate coverage of their market without utilizing professional staff in an uneconomic way. This does not imply that they need "high-pressure" salesmen to survive. Many of these sales people are experienced and knowledgeable about technical appraisal matters and are of valuable assistance in clarifying valuation issues and in helping you specify your appraisal needs. When the time comes to make your decision on an appraiser or firm, however, do not hesitate to request an interview with the relevant professional staff.

Always meet personally the individual appraiser whom you intend to retain or, when dealing with a firm, the appraiser who will be responsible for your assignment. An appraiser is an investigator, a researcher, an analyst, a writer, a lecturer, and possibly a witness. The appraiser may need to interview employees of a target company without revealing the purpose of the investigation, to "separate the wheat from the chaff" in information provided, to interface effectively with your auditors, attorneys, investment bankers, or financial backers. The appraiser may need to interview and request data from the employees of an acquired company at a time when they are least interested in assisting the project.

The appraiser in charge should have the necessary authority within the firm to obtain, and hold, the resources to complete the assignment properly. These resources are primarily professional staff, but can include computer hardware and personnel, technical specialists, and clerical staff. A large engagement can strain these resources and, if your work is displaced by another, larger assignment, quality or timely delivery may suffer.

In any case, the appraiser must provide you with the study results in a concise and understandable form. The only way for you to be comfortable with your professional appraiser in these varied roles is to meet the man or woman personally.

Evaluating the Candidates

Nearly every appraisal requires a varying degree of judgment. The valuation of a painting by an unknown artist would be highly subjective. Even in this case, however, an experienced fine arts appraiser would make a judgment based on such factors as the technical skill of the artist, the current popularity of the style and subject matter, the size of the painting, and the strength of the intended market.

None of these elements, with the exception of size, can be quantified with any degree of precision. However, such a value conclusion should not be classified as a "wild guess." If a group of equally experienced and competent appraisers were to opine on the value of this painting, their conclusions would probably be within a reasonable range. Further, the painting, at auction, would probably bring a price consistent with that range, barring unusual circumstances.

The valuation of a corporate bond is a much less subjective matter. A corporate bond with, as an example, a face value of $1,000, a Standard & Poor's rating of AAA, and a coupon rate of 6.25% can be valued with considerable precision. With a knowledge of current market interest rates and some arithmetic calculations, a value can be derived. Perhaps the essential difference between this and the example of a painting is that the valuation of the bond is the result of having available facts from external public sources and accepted techniques for calculating the present worth of such an investment.

True, there are some assumptions that have to be made. Is the industry within which the company operates in disfavor or enjoying unusual investment popularity? Are there redemption privileges that differ from other bonds on the market? On balance, however, there is much less subjectivity here, and the appraisal client has the opportunity to test the underlying assumptions and weigh their impact on the result.

The qualifications of the appraiser are, then, extremely important. In the case of the painting, they are everything, because a valuation of the work by anyone not qualified becomes an unsupported guess, and you, as the client, have no means to know how good or bad that guess might be. In the case of the bond, there are verifiable facts that are embedded in the judgment and these can be checked and their use in calculations audited. It is therefore essential to investigate the credentials of any appraiser, or appraisal firm, that you intend to utilize. These credentials may take a variety of forms, but there are some essential considerations.

Qualifications.   Individual appraisers' credentials should contain references to:

1.   Work experience, including the number of years as an appraiser and a description of responsibilities (appraiser, supervisor or manager, project manager, partner, principal).

2. Educational background.
3. Clients served.
4. Areas of specialization.
5. Court testimony (including type of case, jurisdiction).
6. Articles written.
7. Supplemental course work, seminars (as instructor or participant).
8. Professional society memberships and designations.

Appraisal firms should provide information that would include at least:

1. Age of the firm.
2. Size of professional staff.
3. Professional disciplines represented.
4. Areas of specialization (geographical as well as type of service).
5. Research facilities.
6. Computer resources (hardware, software, and "people-ware").
7. Client references.
8. Financial resources.

Again, whatever the selection criteria used, the task should be matched to the individual or firm, taking into consideration both ordinary business prudence and the unique qualifications of an individual or firm for a specific assignment. The purely business criteria are those applied in retaining any consultant, whatever the field.

Permanence.   Many appraisal situations last for a long time. An estate or gift tax return may be filed several years before it is audited and it becomes necessary to support values. One wants to be assured that the appraiser, or firm, will be available when that happens.

Financial Resources.   While related to the above, this should be a consideration, especially in large assignments. It takes significant working capital to finance the execution of a large engagement and to *stay with it* until it is complete to everyone's satisfaction. You do not want your engagement to come to "completion" only because the appraiser ran out of capital.

Reputation.   There are relatively few individuals and firms active in the business appraisal field, and therefore it is not difficult to learn something about almost any candidate by inquiring among other professionals or business peers. Use this as a confirming technique rather than a primary criterion.

Creativity.   This may surprise many readers and it is with some trepidation that this criterion is included. Too often, "creative," when used to describe a professional, is a derogatory term—a "creative accountant" makes profits disappear from a tax return; a "creative attorney" finds a case where there isn't one. To say that a business manager should seek a "creative appraiser" is not to be interpreted as a suggestion to find an appraiser who will give the desired conclusion, regardless of the facts. Unfortunately, "creative professionals" (if one can juxtapose those contradictory words) do exist.

"Creativity" refers not to the invention of facts or new theories, but to the imaginative application of tested methods to new situations. New situations, in the form of new properties and new appraisal needs, are constantly arising. Computer software is perhaps 30 years old and appraisals of software only 15. Someone had to apply known valuation principles to the appraisal of a leasehold interest in a satellite transponder. And someone had to be the first to appraise a gene pool or a monoclonal antibody.

Therefore, look for some measure of creativity and some indication that the prospective appraiser will not merely look upon your assignment as just another job, to be ground out like countless previous ones, in the same "cookie cutter" way.

Matching the Assignment and Firm.   Another area of concern addresses those factors that may be unique to an individual or firm and should be measured against a specific appraisal assignment.

Project Management Experience.   Does the firm have experience in assignments of the size contemplated? Is there the capability to correlate the conclusions of various disciplines and/or subcontractors?

Research Capability.   Does the firm have the strength of staff and resources to obtain the necessary information about economic trends, markets, specialized business segments, or technology? Are relationships maintained with experts outside of the appraisal field upon whom the firm can call for assistance?

Computer Resources.   Many appraisal assignments require extensive computer processing and specialized software. When an assignment will require such resources, inquire as to their source, location, and operation. Computer resources under the control of the firm are preferable to those utilized on a contract basis from a third party.

Personnel Qualifications. Specific qualifications have been previously discussed and apply here relative to the "team" that would be assigned to the project.

Specialization. Does the firm have a specific area of concentration? This can be quite valuable if that area coincides with the primary valuation effort or, conversely, a hindrance if the primary valuation effort will have to be accomplished by other than your prime contractor.

Character of Assignment. Some assignments require "brute force," so to speak, and the ability to mobilize a large number of appraisers on short notice. Other assignments must be very carefully planned in order to conform to unusual time schedules. An assignment may call for a high degree of sensitivity or confidentiality or the ability to deal with a contentious situation. Some assignments are sure to end up in court, with the appraiser as expert witness, or being presented to the board of directors of your company.

The following chapters will enable you to evaluate an assignment from the appraiser's point of view, in order to better match an assignment and an appraiser.

Multiple Firms

Although uncommon several years ago, appraisal clients now sometimes consider, and retain, more than one firm on an assignment. This has come about because appraisal assignments are larger (because of bigger businesses) and more complex (because of the "conglomeration" of business). It is also because there are more appraisal firms in existence today and because many of them specialize.

Advantages. These include the ability to complete an assignment more quickly and with a better matching of skills to the engagement.

Disadvantages. These include the possibility of duplicated effort (and fee), inconsistency in methodology, properties or assets "falling through the cracks," and no centralized responsibility.

Suggestions.   If you have a situation in which you believe that retaining more than one firm will be beneficial, consider the following courses of action:

1.   Tell the firm that would otherwise be the single contractor what you are considering, and why, and solicit their response. They may propose to retain special consultants for certain work or commit additional staff in order to satisfy your concerns.

2.   Be "upfront" with all the candidates and make sure they are willing to participate in a team appraisal.

3.   DON'T be your own general contractor. Retain one of the firms to manage the assignment, to write the report, to take responsibility for quality, and to make sure there is consistency. The other firms should be subcontractors to the lead firm.

4.   There should be some logical division of the assignment: by property location; by business segment; by appraisal discipline.

WORKING WITH THE APPRAISER

Retaining the Successful Candidate

Following the decision to retain the consultant, there are a number of issues that must be dealt with before the work can begin.

The Client.   The question of who should be the client often arises. It is not uncommon to have an attorney or law firm as the client in an appraisal. Most often the reason is because the outcome of an appraisal is unknown until the assignment is nearly complete. If the appraisal conclusion turns out to be damaging to a client case, the attorney can cancel the assignment and there will not be evidence in his client's hands inimical to the position the client wishes to take. This strategy may or may not be successful and, of course, it does not alter the course of the valuation work, but it does occur.

There may be other considerations concerning the choice of appraisal client. For example, two clients may be served jointly in a single engagement. At times this is an accommodation to enable two parties to share the cost of the work. At other times it is arranged so that both parties will have input relative to the purpose, assumptions, and data used in the appraisal. On rare occasions, dual clients are adversaries who have agreed to abide by the appraisal conclusion. Obviously, these can be very difficult assignments that require extreme care and discretion so that each side has its "day in court" with the appraiser during the conduct of the work. These same conditions exist when the two clients are not legal adversaries but rather two parties with differing interests, such as buyer and seller.

Within a corporate organization there may be reasons why one entity or another should be the client. The appraisal and work papers are technically the property of the client, and so an operation that is to be sold to an outsider should not be the client if there would be some sensitivity in divulging either the appraisal results or other proprietary information contained within it.

It is therefore important to both appraiser and prospective client that the designation of the legal client be carefully considered, because it establishes an important relationship that may be impractical to change later. The appraiser has a fiduciary responsibility to the client which means that:

1. All working papers are client property, although these are most commonly retained by the appraiser.

2. Valuation conclusions in any form will only be divulged to the client, or to others by client permission.

3. Knowledge acquired by the appraiser during an engagement is confidential.

Contracts. A formal contract with an appraiser or appraisal firm may or may not be advisable. The firm should provide a confirmation letter to you. In fact, most insurance companies that provide errors and omissions insurance to appraisers require such a document. When a governmental body is the client, however, a formal contract may be required as a matter of law.

A letter of confirmation from the appraiser or a letter of acceptance from a client in response to a proposal is the most practical way to do business. Either of these constitutes a legal contract, and the absence of "legalese" enhances the understanding between client and professional, which allows both to accomplish their objectives without undue constraint. A letter of confirmation should include:

1. Identification of the client.
2. Purpose of the appraisal.
3. Premise of value.
4. Appraisal date.
5. Property to be included and excluded.
6. Form and content of the report.
7. Delivery schedule.
8. Fee arrangements.

Clients sometimes propose formal contracts that include penalties for late delivery and/or rewards for early delivery of study conclusions. Such provisions are not recommended. In a contract for the construction of a building, this type of provision may be appropriate because it is easier to verify whether the contract has been fulfilled. For a professional assignment it is much more difficult. Therefore, a "penalty for late delivery" will assure that the appraisal *will* be done, but you, as client, will have the responsibility of determining whether, in fact, the work was completed properly and you may never know for sure until it is too late. It is much better to establish an atmosphere of mutual trust with the professional and omit delivery specifications in the form of penalties and rewards. Instead, meet personally with the responsible professional staff members and assure yourself that they can command the necessary resources within their firm and that they have a commitment that you feel comfortable with. If you do not feel that way, do not retain the firm.

Fees. In Chapter 1 it was noted that appraisers are precluded from accepting fees that are based on a percentage of value concluded or upon the successful outcome of litigation, negotiation, etc. The fee, therefore, will be based upon the magnitude of the work effort.

Typically, an appraiser or appraisal firm will quote fees as *estimates*, comprised of *professional staff time* and a *reimbursement of out-of-pocket costs*.

Fees with respect to professional staff work will vary according to the experience level and qualifications of the individuals assigned. It may be quoted as an hourly amount or a *per diem*. At the time of this writing, *per diems* ranged between $400 and $1,200 for appraisers with 1–3 years' experience and for senior staff, respectively. It is customary for the cost of clerical staff to be included in the quoted professional *per diem*, although in some cases "paraprofessionals" or technicians may be billed in addition.

If testimony is expected, the appraiser will often quote a basic fee for the appraisal report with subsequent time on a *per diem* basis. This is because time required for evaluating the testimony of others and preparing for and providing direct testimony is not under the appraiser's control.

The reimbursement of out-of-pocket expenses usually includes the cost of travel and living expenses incurred when professionals are away from their home location, as well as the cost of computer time, postage, duplication of reports, telephone charges, and the like. The largest element of this cost is usually travel and living expenses and, while the days of first-class air travel are gone for most firms, out-of-pocket expenses usually are approximately 15 to 20 percent of the total fee. The client can do little to reduce significantly this portion of the total cost. Attempts to utilize corporate aircraft or accommodations or to place restrictions on certain elements of expense may well result in excessive staff time and be counterproductive.

Expect to be billed *per diem* rates at the high end of the range if you desire specific individuals to work on a project,, or if the delivery requirements will disrupt the near-term work schedule of the firm. Expect higher *per diems* if the case will definitely involve litigation or lead to a possible "landmark case," because the appraiser will recognize the exposure and subject the work to more research and executive scrutiny than would otherwise be the case.

On the other side, one could expect lower than normal fees if several firms are competing for the assignment or if it is highly desirable because of the professional visibility that might result. A large and/or complex engagement successfully concluded is a professional's best means for business development. The concept of supply and demand applies to consulting as well as to other businesses, even though consultants would prefer not to recognize it.

Some other conditions that can result in higher or lower fees include the following:

HIGHER
1. Multiple small locations.
2. Multiple legal entities (subsidiaries, divisions, minority interests) within the property.
3. Many dissimilar product lines or business segments.
4. An adversarial position wherein data will be difficult to obtain.
5. A start-up enterprise or emerging product lines.
6. Incomplete accounting data available.
7. Appraisal "as of" date well in the past.

LOWER
1. Single location, enterprise, product.
2. Good preparation for the appraiser's visit(s).
3. Property descriptions accumulated and complete.
4. Timely access to key personnel.
5. Informative and detailed accounting data available.

Can the fee be negotiated? The answer is "yes." The real question is "How much?"

Estimated fees for a given engagement should vary only within a relatively narrow range *if* the specifications remain the same. If the appraisers or appraisal firms proposing to do the work are competent, they should see the work effort in much the same light, and their fee quotations will be very similar. When there are significant differences in quoted fee, it is usually because of a difference of opinion about the *specifications* for the assignment or because of a difference in the *appraisal techniques* to be utilized. When evaluating disparate fee quotations, the prospective client is well advised to clarify the differences before retaining a firm that may quote the lowest-appearing fee. A client is always well advised to have a full understanding of the appraisal requirements and the alternatives for meeting them. No one wants to pay for butter when margarine will suffice, but when butter is required, one must be assured of receiving it.

In the chapters that follow, different value premises, methods, and techniques will be discussed. Part of these discussions will center around the cost impact of different appraisal techniques and they will provide some assistance in measuring the cost/benefit relationships that exist.

If the specifications or techniques are clear, but one still has some discomfort relative to authorizing an engagement on the basis of a fee *estimate*, there are several courses of action available. One can simply request a fee quote on a maximum, or not to exceed, basis. Another option is to structure the engagement into several discrete tasks with an individual fee quotation for each. These tasks can be authorized individually and monitored on that basis. This may cost somewhat more in the overall engagement because of inefficiencies produced by starting and stopping the work at each phase, but prevents a massive fee overrun. It is better to negotiate a total fee and closely monitor the progress of the engagement. There is an additional technique that can be very effective in "scoping" an engagement and its fee: authorize a *preliminary study*, which is a quick, "mini-appraisal" at a modest fee. There are two benefits in this technique: first, because the appraiser receives better information about the property and information available, a more precise estimate of fee can be made, and, second, a rough estimate of value can be obtained.

This technique is especially useful when a particular course of action depends on the appraisal conclusion, such as the decision to sell or buy a property. One can decide to go forward with the full appraisal based on the early indication of value produced in the preliminary.

Many experienced appraisers do a "preliminary," whether authorized or not. As a practical matter, client expectations are almost always known at the outset. If it becomes obvious, early in the work, that the expectations are unrealistic, then it is better to conclude the engagement before both a higher fee and unpleasant value conclusions lead to hard feelings.

There is, in fact, no standard work effort (and, therefore, fee) associated with a particular appraisal assignment. One could, for example, appraise a residence for a fee of $25 or $2,500. For the $25 fee, the appraiser would drive by and telephone the conclusion. For the $2,500 fee, the appraiser would make a market, income, and cost analysis and provide a written report. Each has its place and purpose, and *so long as* appraiser and client clearly understand both, professional service is rendered. In practice, the appraisal of real estate is more standardized than any other area, so perhaps the above example is oversimplified.

This situation is very real, however, in appraisals of a business enterprise or the tangible and intangible assets that comprise it. Later chapters discuss the appraisal of these types of property so that the reader will be equipped to match appraisal techniques and work effort with appraisal objectives, thereby assuring that the fee for an appraisal assignment is commensurate with its purpose.

Payment.   Expect to be invoiced during the progress of the engagement unless the work is expected to be completed within a month or so. If this arrangement is not satisfactory, it should be discussed at the beginning of the assignment. A retainer of 25 to 50 percent of the total fee may be requested unless previous work or a client's credit standing makes this unnecessary.

Getting Started

Liaison.   Someone in the client organization should be given the responsibility to act as liaison with the appraiser or appraisal firm. This person should be thoroughly familiar with the property and the eventual use of the valuation. The appraiser's requests for access to properties, information, and personnel are channelled through this person. This is the most efficient way to handle these requests and provides the client, as well, with a means to monitor the progress and techniques of the appraiser.

Security.   It is not unusual to request an appraiser to execute confidentiality agreements on behalf of the firm and/or individual professionals. Access to sensitive information is often necessary to complete an assignment, and such a safeguard is both reasonable and prudent. No appraiser or firm should have any reluctance to such a provision. If governmental clearances are required, that fact should be made known at the outset so that compliance can be arranged. Client wishes regarding photographs of the property should be communicated to the appraiser.

Starting the Project.   Previously discussed was the efficacy of scheduling a "kick-off" meeting with your principal managers as well as those of the property or business to be appraised, if different. If this is not practical, memoranda should be sent to affected managers explaining the project and enlisting their cooperation. Letters of introduction can also be given to the appraiser to facilitate later contact.

In all but very straightforward assignments, the appraiser should submit a written request in advance for information that will be needed at the time of field investigation.

Access.   On-site visits by the appraiser will need to be arranged and, in most cases, some working space for the appraisal staff will be required. Special arrangements may have to be made for access to hazardous areas or to locations requiring special dress (clean rooms, laboratories, operating rooms),or for special timing (nights, weekends, or between shifts).

"Freezing" Data.   When the appraiser requires records that, in the normal course of business, are continually changing, it is essential that this information be captured as of the appraisal date. As an example, it may be necessary to prepare financial statements as of a date that is not a normal accounting cut-off date. A list of customers, subscribers, suppliers, advertisers, or borrowers may have to be extracted from a continually changing database. This is especially critical with computer-resident records, where it may be very difficult to reconstruct the population of records that existed at an earlier date.

Checking Progress

Except on a short, one- or two-week, assignment, an appraisal client should establish the means to monitor the progress of the work. This may necessitate meetings with the responsible appraiser or written progress reports. In this way, the client is aware of where the appraisal staff is located physically as well as in the assignment, and who is on the job. Just as important, one becomes aware of delays in providing access or information to the appraiser so that action can be taken to prevent deterioration in the quality or delivery of the product.

Concluding the Assignment

Appraisal conclusions should be delivered to the client in several stages: (1) preliminary totals, (2) draft report, and (3) final report.

Preliminary totals.   These can be transmitted in written or verbal form and serve two purposes:

1.   To provide early conclusions so that the client does not have to wait for a narrative report.
2.   To provide the client with an opportunity to "respond" to the values.

Often, preliminary totals do not contain as much detail (such as values by property classification or individual location) as the final report. Client time requirements may dictate the delivery of two levels of conclusions in increasing degrees of precision.

In a complex engagement, preliminary totals are most often presented in a meeting with client management. This allows for a fuller explanation of the value conclusions and methodologies.

IT IS IMPORTANT TO NOTE THAT the purpose of preliminary totals is *not* to negotiate the value conclusions with the appraiser, but, in part, to receive client input, whether or not that input has any effect on the conclusion. A homeowner's appeal of a property tax assessment is an analogous event. The homeowner is given the opportunity to present facts that may or may not have been considered by the assessor or to point out errors of fact.

Draft Report.   This is an otherwise complete narrative report that is submitted for client review, again not to negotiate the appraiser's opinions, but to clarify matters of fact, if necessary.

Final Report.   This report reflects client comments to the extent that the appraiser feels appropriate and typically includes:

1. A transmittal letter.
2. An executive summary.
3. Narrative section.
4. Exhibits, which would include financial data, statistical studies, schedules, and photographs.
5. Appendices, which might include appraiser qualifications and limiting conditions.
6. Inventory, especially if tangible property is extensive and requires a voluminous listing.
7. Computer records of property, such as lists of fixed assets, customers, subscribers, or advertisers.

Appraisers are becoming more attuned to the use of computers, especially in the valuation of the tangible and intangible assets of a business enterprise, and are prepared to provide their appraisal conclusions in that form to clients who have the capability to utilize this record form.

Chapter 10 presents an annotated sample report to show the essential parts of an appraisal narrative.

3

WHEN VALUATION SERVICES ARE NEEDED

Appraisals are nearly always performed in response to a specific need, and most of these needs arise from outside the business involved. These needs typically relate to either an *actual* transfer of property (such as a purchase, sale, or gift) or a *presumed* transfer (to serve as the basis of a property settlement or taxation).

Most appraisal requirements can be classified as follows:

Accounting-related requirements arise when *values* rather than *costs* are needed to reflect properly a transaction according to generally accepted accounting principles (GAAP).

Taxation-related valuations are made to establish the *basis* on which some form of tax or deduction from tax is to be calculated.

Financing-related valuations may be required to establish the amount of collateral securing a loan or as the basis for a fairness opinion in connection with a sale of stock in the public market.

Litigation-related appraisals may be made to arrive at a settlement between joint property owners, to form the basis of damage claims, to be part of a utility rate proceeding, or to establish a position in a property condemnation.

Management-related valuations can form the basis for agreements between a company and its employees and/or stockholders for intracorporate asset transfers, for decisions as to the sale or purchase of property, and for use by a board of directors in evaluating offers for the purchase of their company.

Each of these classifications is discussed below. Since appraisals for accounting and tax reasons are the most frequent, they are discussed in more detail.

ACCOUNTING

There are a number of circumstances in which *values* rather than *costs* are utilized in accounting statements prepared according to GAAP.

Acquisitions

In 1970, opinions 16 and 17 of the Accounting Principles Board (of the American Institute of Certified Public Accountants) became effective. These opinions, commonly referred to as APB 16 and APB 17, covered many issues related to the purchase of one company by another and how such a business combination should be reflected on the books of the surviving business.

Briefly stated, APB 16 provides that an acquisition of a business enterprise can be accounted for as a "pooling of interests" or as a "purchase." In a pooling, the recorded assets and liabilities of the individual companies are consolidated to become the recorded assets and liabilities of the combined corporation at their historical, cost-based amounts.

The accounting for an acquisition treated as a purchase is similar to that of a purchase of a single asset except that the "cost" (the price of the entire business enterprise) is attributable to a large group of assets.

When the consideration paid (price) is other than cash, the cost basis for ongoing accounting may be determined by the fair value of assets distributed, such as marketable securities, properties, or liabilities assumed. In this way, the overall cost basis of the assets acquired is established. When assets are acquired as a group, the cost is allocated to the individual assets in the group on the basis of their fair value.

APB 17 addresses the proper accounting treatment of intangible assets acquired from individuals or as part of the purchase of a business enterprise. When an intangible asset is purchased separately from a business combination, its cost is recorded as an asset. When specifically identifiable intangible assets are purchased as part of a business combination, their cost, for future accounting purposes, is represented by their value at the time of acquisition and they are amortized over their remaining economic life. Goodwill, similarly acquired, is recorded as the residual between the total purchase price and the identified assets and liabilities assumed and is amortized over its estimated economic life, but no longer than 40 years.

These requirements translate into a need to establish the fair value of the various types of assets acquired and liabilities assumed with the enterprise. Enter the appraiser.

The "plant, property, and equipment" of the acquired company must be appraised, together with any identifiable intangible assets such as contracts, patents, and franchises, whether or not they were recorded on the balance sheet of the acquired company. Other balance sheet assets may also require appraisal as indicated in the following schedule:

Classification	New Cost Basis
Assets	
Current Assets	
Marketable securities	NRV
Accounts receivable	PV
Inventories	
Raw material	RC
Work in process	$SP - (C + D + P)$
Finished goods	$SP - (C + D + P)$
Fixed Assets	
Permanent use	RCNLD
Temporary use	$NRV - D$
For sale	NRV
Intangible Assets	AV
Other Assets	AV
Goodwill	RES
Liabilities	
Current Liabilities	PV
Long-term Liabilities	PV
Accruals	PV
Other Liabilities	PV

> NRV: Current net realizable value, or ex-
> pected selling price less selling costs. PV:
> Present value at the current interest rate
> commensurate with the risk of realizing the
> income. RC: Current replacement cost. SP:
> Selling price. C: Completion cost. D: Dis-
> posal cost. P: Profit. RCNLD: Current re-
> placement cost less depreciation. AV: Ap-
> praised value, or fair market value. RES:
> Residual between the total purchase price
> and the value of identified assets and liabil-
> ities assumed.

The difference between the value of these assets and the purchase price is deemed to be goodwill. These values serve, then, as the basis for an allocation of the purchase price to the assets acquired, and this allocation will become part of the opening balance sheet of the surviving company. Value, rather than cost, is the basis for future depreciation calculations and the determination of stockholders' equity.

Leased Property

Statement 13 of the Financial Accounting Standards Board, Accounting for Leases, is based on the principle that:

> . . . a lease that transfers substantially all of the benefits and risks of ownership
> should be accounted for as the acquisition of an asset and the incurrence of an
> obligation by the lessee (a capital lease) . . .[1]

FASB 13 is a complex document, dealing with many accounting issues. Valuation issues center around some of the criteria used to determine whether a given lease arrangement should be accounted as a capital lease. These criteria include:

1. The lease contains an option to purchase the leased property at a *bargain price*.
2. The lease term is equal to or greater than 75 percent of the *estimated economic life* of the leased property.

3. The present value of rental and other minimum lease payments equals or exceeds 90 percent of the *fair value* of the leased property.

Having participated in the decision as to whether a lease arrangement should be considered a capital lease, the appraiser may again be called upon to make further determinations, since:

> The amount to be recorded by the lessee as an asset and an obligation under a capital lease is the lesser of the present value of the rental and other minimum lease payments or the fair value of the leased property.[2]

There are occasions, of course, when the *purchase price* of property leased immediately after purchase may be synonymous with *fair value*, as defined in FASB 13. In that case, an appraisal may not be required. The discussion in chapters that follow will explain the differences among cost, price, and fair market value.

Property Records

There are situations in which appraisal techniques are used to calculate historical costs which have been recorded erroneously or in a form that is not practical.

The amounts shown under "Plant, property, and equipment" on a typical balance sheet are themselves a summarization of detailed records of asset purchases and disposals over the years that a company has been in business. Such a detailed record for an individual machine might show, for example:

1. Description.
2. Manufacturer.
3. Model.
4. Serial number.
5. Attachments.
6. Prime mover.
7. Original cost.
8. Year of purchase.
9. Annual book depreciation expense.
10. Annual tax depreciation expense.

11. Accumulated book depreciation.
12. Accumulated tax depreciation.

A continuing property record (CPR) in a large company will contain many individual records and will undergo constant change as the equipment needs of the firm change. Building additions are constructed and portions of buildings are razed. Whole production lines of machinery may be purchased and added to the record as one line item, whereas another machine might receive a new motor which would also be recorded as a separate item. It is not at all uncommon for a CPR to become a "hodgepodge" after a number of years of activity.

In order for the company's balance sheet to reflect accurately the property that is actually being used, it is necessary to record disposals of property and remove their original cost and depreciation reserve from the books and tax records. The company's auditors also need to satisfy themselves as to the accuracy of the CPR. Neither of these objectives can be accomplished if property items are not clearly identified in the CPR. In this situation, it may be necessary to perform a physical inventory of the entire property and reconcile the inventory to the existing CPR, creating a new record with meaningful descriptive data and purging the CPR of unrecorded disposals.

There are appraisers who specialize in property record work and are skilled in inventory procedures, in building and equipment nomenclature, in reconciliation calculations, and in the preparation of a useful property record system. They are also knowledgeable of the accounting and tax impact of this work. The appraiser's knowledge of current as well as historical values can be essential in the reconciliation process.

Depreciation

Depreciation is a term that has two distinct meanings. For the appraiser, "depreciation" most often refers to *a loss in value* suffered by property from a variety of causes. This use of the word is discussed in a subsequent section. To an accountant, depreciation refers to an *allocation of cost*. When an asset is purchased and is expected to be useful for several years, it would be a distortion of the financial statements to reflect the asset cost entirely in the period when the expenditure was made. The cost of acquiring the asset is therefore spread over the time it will be used. For example, when a building is purchased, its cost is allocated evenly over the future years during which it will be occupied:

$$\frac{\text{Original Cost}}{\text{Useful Life}} = \frac{\$1,000,000}{40 \text{ Years}} = \$25,000 \text{ per year}$$

As an accounting concept, then, depreciation is a means to allocate the cost of *physical property* over its useful life. When the cost of intangible property or other expenditures, such as the cost of organizing a new division or company or developing a new tradename or logo, are to be allocated to future periods, it is called amortization, although the basic techniques are the same.

So far this discussion has dealt with cost. Where does value enter the picture? Since the objective of accounting depreciation is to reflect, as accurately as possible, the true cost of property within a business, it must also recognize that some property has residual value at the end of its normal life. The amount that must be recovered in depreciation is, then, the original cost *less* the amount realized in disposing of the property. As an example, assume that a company has an established practice of keeping automobiles for three years. A three-year-old auto has some value on the used market, however, so it is not necessary to recover the full original cost in depreciation. The property has a *salvage* value, equal to its selling price in the used market. If it is the company's practice to sell used autos itself, by advertising and handling the transfer, then some *disposal costs* will be incurred. The difference between the selling price and disposal costs is *net salvage*, which should be deducted from the original cost when computing depreciation expense. Thus, *value* enters into the depreciation equation.

Because appraisers constantly deal with the consideration of *economic useful life* (the period during which an asset can contribute to the earning power of an enterprise), they are often called upon to assist in the estimation of *depreciable life*, or *capital recovery period*, for accounting purposes. This too will be a subject covered in later sections, but it is mentioned here to emphasize the common ground between the concept of economic useful life used by the appraiser and the allocation of cost required by the accountant.

Financial Reporting and Changing Prices

The accounting profession has for many years attempted to devise a method that would overcome the instability in financial statements caused by changes in the purchasing power of the dollar. The problem has been studied by various accounting policy bodies since the late 1940s. In March 1976, the Securities and Exchange Commission issued Accounting Series Release

(ASR) 190, requiring certain publicly held companies to disclose replacement cost information about inventories, cost of sales, productive capacity, and depreciation.

In September 1979, the FASB issued Statement 33, "Financial Reporting and Changing Prices." This statement required certain large, publicly held enterprises to report the effect of inflation and changes in the prices of certain types of assets as supplementary information in their published financial statements. These requirements concern the current cost of inventory; property, plant, and equipment; cost of goods sold; depreciation; depletion and amortization expense. Current costs may be developed in several ways:

A. Indexation
  1. Externally generated price indexes for the class of goods or services being measured.
  2. Internally generated price indexes for the class of goods or services being measured.
B. Direct pricing
  1. Current invoice prices.
  2. Vendor's price lists or other quotations or estimates.
  3. Standard manufacturing costs that reflect current costs.

FASB 33 further requires that, for assets having a "recoverable amount" lower than current cost, the recoverable amount shall be used as the measure of the assets and of the expense associated with the use or sale of the assets. If an asset or group of assets is to be sold, the recoverable amount is equal to the expected proceeds of the sale, net of selling costs. If an asset or group of assets will not be sold, the recoverable amount is measured by the net present value of future cash flows expected to be derived from using the asset on a continuing basis. This methodology is discussed at length in Chapter 4 as the "Income Approach."

This discussion of FASB 33 is not intended to be a comprehensive presentation of its requirements, but rather to point out another use of *value* information in accounting statements. As subsequent chapters show, the use of price indexes, current unit costs, and present value techniques are basic to valuation and anyone faced with complying with FASB 33 should utilize the services of a professional appraiser.

In June 1986, the FASB announced that compliance with Statement 33 requirements will be voluntary in reporting financial results for fiscal years ending after 15 March 1987.

TAXATION

There are more appraisal requirements driven by taxes than any other cause. These are generally related to taxes on income (state and federal) and on the value of property.

Income tax laws, both state and federal, are, of course, constantly changing. As this is written, the provisions of the Tax Reform Act of 1986 (TRA), are about to become effective. Many of these provisions will have a significant effect on the need for valuation services. Two of these provisions, the elimination of Investment Tax Credit and the repeal of the "General Utilities Doctrine," will have the immediate effect of reducing valuation requirements. However, these tax issues are discussed because in the future these provisions, or some like them, may return to the federal tax code.

Investment Tax Credit

In 1962, Investment Tax Credit (ITC) became part of the Internal Revenue Code of 1954 (IRC) as Section 38. This section, as it was enacted and later extensively modified, is very complex, and a complete description of it would be lengthy and beyond the scope of this book. Although it is not a "value-based" concept, appraisers have been very much involved in ITC-related analyses.

As enacted, Section 38 provided that a taxpayer who invested in tangible personal property, other tangible property (*not* buildings or structural components) which is an integral part of a manufacturing process, or elevators and escalators could claim a tax credit of 7 percent of cost in the year of investment.

ITC was suspended in late 1966 to early 1967 and was terminated by the Tax Reform Act of 1969. It was reinstated, as a "job development credit," in 1971. Beginning with the Tax Reduction Act of 1975, and until the Tax Equity and Fiscal Responsibility Act of 1982 (TEFRA), ITC regulations were modified several times. The Tax Reform Act of 1984 attempted to simplify the rules, and, finally, the Tax Reform Act of 1986 repealed ITC. Taxpayer deductions under the provisions of Section 38 have been the subject of many Revenue Rulings and Tax Court cases because of the "on again, off again" situation and because of the necessity to interpret what was and was not "qualifying property."

It would appear, on the surface, that the application of such a provision would be easy—obtain the cost of qualifying property, multiply by .07, and the resulting credit against income tax would be obtained. It was this simple for some types of property, such as a lathe, a truck, or a boiler. It was much less clear in the case of equipment that provided temperature and humidity control in a computer room or of the structural part of a building that was required to support heavy machinery or an overhead crane (keeping in mind that the "building" structure was excluded).

In these cases, if accurate *and* detailed cost records are available on the segments of construction, the segregation of qualifying and non-qualifying property is clear. When this is not the case, an appraiser is needed. It becomes necessary to extract the costs of qualifying property from a lump-sum contract price. In the absence of detailed price quotes or invoices, it is necessary to develop the then-current costs of various construction elements, because the contractor has no need to set out the costs of property segments that have different *tax* treatment. The contractor's requirements are quite different and usually relate to the costs of building elements that are related to subcontractor responsibilities. Thus, the contractor is concerned with the subcontractor's price for plumbing in total, *not* the cost of plumbing for laboratories as opposed to bathrooms.

Acquisitions

As with GAAP, there are regulations in IRC that apply to the acquisition of one company by another and to the method for determining the tax basis of the surviving entity. There are non-taxable transactions and taxable ones. In a non-taxable transaction, the tax basis of the acquired company is carried over without change, similar to "pooling" as previously described. In a taxable transaction, a purchase takes place (either deemed or actual) that triggers taxable events, such as depreciation recapture, or the calculation of gains or losses for the acquired business, or a change in tax basis for the acquiring entity. Both buyer and seller have a requirement to distribute the exchange consideration to the individual assets acquired (or sold).

Section 334(b)(2) of the IRC for many years governed a particular type of taxable transaction involving the purchase of substantially all of the stock of a company and a subsequent liquidation of the company into the acquiring corporation. TEFRA replaced Section 334(b)(2) with Section 338. The Tax Reform Act of 1986 made further changes in the regulations applying to this form of acquisition.

The "General Utilities Doctrine," so called because it came from a Tax Court decision involving General Utilities & Operating Co. V. Helvering (296 U.S. 200 1935) was embodied in IRC Sections 311 and 336 and was effectively repealed as part of TRA (Section 631), effective 1 January 1987. Under the former rules, a liquidating corporation did not recognize a taxable gain or loss on the distribution of its assets to shareholders in the liquidation. A liquidation of this type was often a part of corporate acquisition strategy. A corporation would purchase all of the stock of another corporation and would liquidate the company, distributing the assets to itself (as sole stockholder) so that, under other IRC rules (Section 338), it could reflect the fair market value of those assets rather than their former cost less accumulated depreciation as the new tax basis. Since the fair market value of the assets would often exceed the former tax basis, deductions for depreciation in the future would be greater than otherwise. In addition, intangible assets, to the extent that they could be identified, valued, and assigned a remaining life, became amortizable and further increased deductions from taxable income following such an acquisition.

This concept is illustrated in Figure 3.1. The left column represents the purchase consideration and the right column the appraised values of assets acquired. The center column is the purchase consideration allocated to the assets appraised.

When a new tax basis was established under Section 338, a taxable sale of assets was deemed to have occurred and certain gains had to be recognized. The taxes due on these gains (primarily in the form of depreciation and ITC recapture) were often outweighed by the advantage of the depreciation and amortization increase, and so this form of acquisition was a popular tax strategy. With the repeal of the General Utilities Doctrine, the gains on the deemed sale would be taxed twice and it appears that there will be far fewer cases in which electing a Section 338 liquidation will be advantageous.

A review of the primary elements of a Section 338 election reveals where the valuation issues are. Temporary Regulations, Section 338(b)-2T(b) describe four asset classifications:

Class I—Cash, demand deposits, and similar accounts in banks, savings and loan associations, and other similar depository institutions.

Class II—Certificates of deposit, U.S. government securities, marketable stock or securities, and foreign currency.

Class III—All assets (other than Class I, II, or IV assets) both tangible and intangible, whether or not depreciable, depletable, or amortizable.

Class IV—Intangible assets in the nature of goodwill and going concern value.

FIGURE 3.1   Allocation of Purchase Consideration

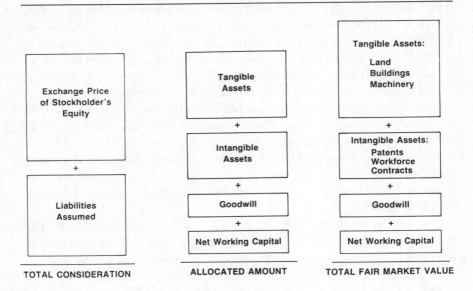

The Temporary Regulations further specified that a residual method would be used to determine the tax basis of the assets deemed purchased under a Section 338 election. The purchase price is first allocated to Class I assets at their face amount (equal to their fair market value). The remainder is then allocated to Class II and III assets according to their fair market values. The remaining purchase price is assigned to Class IV assets. This is the essence of the process and an oversimplification of what can be a very complex procedure.

The critical issues are in the determination of the fair market value of the Class III assets (since the value of Class I and II assets should be reasonably easy to determine) and in evaluation of the amount of residual going to Class IV as to whether it is reasonable and whether there is potentially any duplication with Class III assets.

The TRA also contains a provision that extends the allocation technique described above to *all* acquisitions of assets that are part of a going concern. As an example, if a corporation purchases all of the assets of a company (as opposed to buying its capital stock), it must allocate the purchase price as outlined above, *and* the new law authorizes the issuance of regulations requiring that the allocation must be agreed to by both buyer and seller, *and* that the amounts allocated to goodwill and going concern elements must be disclosed to the Internal Revenue Service (IRS). This does not necessarily mean that the IRS will agree with the allocation, but merely that it will be aware of it. This differs from previous conditions in two ways: first, consistency between a buyer's and seller's allocations was formerly not mandatory and may or may not have been compared by the IRS, and second, if an allocation was agreed to by both buyer and seller, it was presumed to have some validity since their motivations were opposed. The seller desired a maximum allocation to goodwill in order to pay capital gains taxes at a lower rate, and the buyer desired to maximize allocation to fixed assets in order to achieve the largest depreciation deduction.

Depreciation

There has probably been more change in depreciable lives for federal tax purposes than in any other part of the IRC. For many years, tax depreciation was based on "facts and circumstances," with each taxpayer faced with the necessity, if called upon, to defend the depreciable life being used for various classes of property. "Bulletin F," published in 1920 and revised in 1931 and 1942, provided normal lives for 2,700 types of depreciable assets. Treasury Decision 4422 established that the burden of proof rested with the taxpayer.

In 1954, with the enactment of the Internal Revenue Code, Congress recognized the importance of depreciation in the calculation of income taxes for capital-intensive U.S. industry and therefore its potential use as a means to legislate the economy. The IRC introduced methods of accelerated depreciation intended to speed the tax-free recovery of property cost and therefore fuel the economy and new capital investment. Since then there has been continual change in both depreciation methods and allowable lives. The Economic Recovery Tax Act (ERTA) introduced the Accelerated Cost Recovery System (ACRS) and the TRA has modified it substantially.

Valuation techniques come into play here as they did with ITC—in establishing the proper depreciation base for the various classes of property in a "lump" investment. For example, a taxpayer might authorize the construction of a manufacturing facility on a "turnkey" basis. The total cost of the project will include many classes of assets, such as land, site work, land improvements, building structures, and machinery and equipment.

The lump-sum cost of the facility must be allocated to the asset classifications shown above *and* to the individual assets within each classification in order to establish the basis for depreciating them according to the current regulations and accounting for their eventual disposal (recapture and capital gains provisions of Sections 1245 and 1250). These important segregations of property can be made using appraisal techniques and information about the current costs of construction and installation. Often, no amount of accounting analysis of contractor invoices or purchase documents is sufficient to extract this information in a meaningful way.

An electrical contractor, for example, rarely segregates the various costs for installing yard lighting, power-feed wiring and switchgear used for machinery, building lighting, or special circuits for a computer or furnace. These investments may have very different treatment as to depreciable life and taxation on disposal, and therefore there can be significant tax benefits in a proper segregation of their cost.

Casualty Losses

Section 165 of the IRC allows a deduction for losses not compensated by insurance or other means. One measure of loss is the decline in the fair market value of the property involved. The regulations (Section 165-7(a)(2)(i) provide:

> In determining the amount of loss deductible under this section, the fair market value of the property immediately before and immediately after the casualty shall generally be ascertained by competent appraisal. This appraisal must recognize the effects of any general market decline affecting undamaged as well as damaged property which may occur simultaneously with the casualty, in order that any deduction under this section shall be limited to the actual loss resulting from damage to the property.

In Publication 334, "Tax Guide for Small Business," the IRS states further:

> *Appraisals*. The difference between the fair market value of property immediately before a casualty or theft and immediately afterwards should be determined by a competent appraisal. The appraiser's knowledge of sales of comparable property and conditions in the area, knowledge of your property before and after the casualty, and method of ascertaining the amount of the loss are important elements for proving a casualty loss.

Employee Stock Ownership Plans

The Employee Retirement Income Security Act of 1974 (ERISA) established a particular form of a qualified stock bonus plan known as an Employee Stock

Ownership Plan (ESOP). In such a plan, investments are primarily in the stock of the employer, and distributions must be in shares of employer stock. Under Section 409(h) of IRC, a distributee has a "put" option whereby the employer must repurchase stock under a fair valuation formula. This provision creates a market for stock which is not publicly traded and which would therefore be marketable only at a heavy discount or not at all. For a publicly traded company, a participating employee can receive the distribution in company stock which can be sold in the open market when desired.

Valuation issues are very important, both to owner/employer and employee participants in an ESOP. The owner is able to claim a tax deduction on stock contributed to an ESOP, and if that deduction is based on a price higher than the stock's true value, a disallowance may result. An employee participant who exercises a "put" option and sells shares back to the plan at a price less than their fair market value could bring suit against the employer or the plan.

In addition, each plan has a trustee who has a fiduciary responsibility to purchase company stock, from either owner or other sources, at its "true value." The trustee may also be called upon to participate in decisions relative to leveraging the ESOP in order to purchase shares from outside sources or to recommend the sale of shares pursuant to an offer to buy the company.

These issues are obviously most critical in the case of stock that is not publicly traded (closely held). Recognizing this, Congress modified the ESOP provisions in TRA to specify that an independent appraiser must perform all valuations of employer securities if those securities are not tradable on an established securities market (Section 401(a)(28(C)).

There are a number of appraisal issues that are not specifically addressed in the IRC relative to ESOPs and which have been the subject of uncertainty among valuation professionals, most of whom have relied on the valuation considerations set out in Revenue Ruling 59-60, but certain factors relating to discounts and premiums are not yet clear. These factors are discussed in a subsequent chapter.

Charitable Contributions

Section 170(a)(1) of IRC is the general authority for tax deductions of charitable contributions. This rule allows both individuals and corporations to deduct an amount equal to the fair market value of property donated to a charitable organization. Fair market value is defined as:

. . . the price at which the property would change hands between a willing
buyer and a willing seller, neither being under any compulsion to buy or sell
and both having reasonable knowledge of relevant facts. (IRC 170A-1(c)(2)

Valuations of contributed property have been the central issue in much litigation between taxpayers and the government. Most of these cases concerned the value of property that had appreciated in value in the hands of
the donor during some period of ownership prior to the donation. Revenue
Rulings 79-419, 79-256, 80-69, and 80-223 discuss some significant cases. In
the Economic Recovery Tax Act of 1981 (ERTA), Section 6659 was added to
the Code, providing for penalties when tax is understated because of over-
valuation. TEFRA made these penalties more stringent. The Tax Reform
Act of 1984 added more teeth to Section 6659.

At present, charitable contributions of property in excess of $5,000 gener-
ally require a qualified appraisal which must be attached to the tax return.
When the donation is in the form of non-publicly traded securities, the
threshold is $10,000. A "qualified appraisal" is described as one:

1. Made not earlier than 60 days before the date of the contribution.
2. Prepared by a "qualified appraiser."
3. Not involving a prohibited type of appraisal fee.
4. Received by the donor before the tax return date.

A "qualified appraiser" must include as part of the appraisal summary provided to the taxpayer a statement that he/she is publicly known as an appraiser, is qualified to appraise the subject property, and is aware that a
fraudulent overstatement of value may subject the appraiser to civil penalties. A "qualified appraiser" also cannot be:

1. A donor or taxpayer receiving any deduction for the subject property.
2. A party to the transaction in which the donor acquired the subject
    property.
3. Someone employed by the donor or connected with the original sale
    of the subject property.
4. Someone who has a relationship with one of the above persons similar
    to that of an employee or which would cast reasonable doubt on the
    ability to be impartial.
5. Compensated by a fee based either on the value determined or the
    amount of the claimed tax deduction.
6. The donee of the subject property.

The appraisal summary to be included with the tax return is on Form 8283 and is signed by both taxpayer and appraiser. Other information to be included describes the property fully and provides additional information about the donor, donee, and appraiser.

Estates and Gifts

For federal tax purposes the basis of taxation of property transferred as part of an estate and by means of a gift is the same, although the actual tax calculation is different. There can be significant differences in the handling of these issues at the state level, however.

Fair market value, as previously defined in the discussion of charitable contributions, is the basis for estate and gift tax valuations. The type of property can be varied and its appraisal may require a number of appraisal disciplines. The taxation of gifts and estates can be quite complex and there should nearly always be an attorney experienced in this practice involved in such a case. Because the results of an appraisal will most often be subject to scrutiny by tax authorities and/or be a part of litigation, it is common for the appraiser to be retained by an attorney. At the beginning of the assignment, the appraiser contracts with the attorney as the client, in the role of consultant. In this way, the appraisal conclusions can be shielded from discovery in subsequent litigation in the event they are inimical to the client's position, whether the client is a taxpayer or a governmental body.

From the appraiser's point of view, there is nothing unique about a valuation for estate or gift tax purposes. This area of practice has, in fact, contributed considerably to the appraiser's body of knowledge about the valuation of closely held stock. Because the valuation of closely held stock arises many times in estate tax matters it has been the subject of many court cases between taxpayer and taxing authority. Consequently, many of the valuation concepts discussed in Chapter 4 had their origin in Tax Court.

Many valuations are undertaken for the purpose of estate planning and, again, these often concern business interests. As an example, the founder of a closely held business enterprise who typically owns essentially all of the common stock and voting control of the company often desires to pass control of the company to other family members and at the same time limit the size of his estate. One technique used to accomplish this is to recapitalize the company, establishing a new class of preferred stock. The value of preferred stock, because of its particular rights of ownership, fluctuates within a rather narrow band. The founder then exchanges common stock for preferred, thus "freezing" the value of his estate. A gift of the common stock is made to the other family members who will receive the appreciation in value of the common stock in the years to come (if the business prospers!). In this case, a valuation is advisable to insure that the values of the preferred stock received and the value of the common exchanged are well supported in order to avoid unexpected taxes levied at a subsequent review.

The concept of "estate freezing" is illustrated in Figure 3.2, which shows how the rights of ownership are divided.

The simplest form of "estate freeze" involves a recapitalization of a single business entity and is illustrated in Figure 3.3.

Where there are various types of assets to be combined in such a transaction, this can be accomplished through either a holding company or by means of a partnership, as illustrated in Figures 3.4 and 3.5.

Property Taxes

Property (*ad valorem*) taxes are levied by local governments and, in some cases, states. They are taxes based on the *value* of property which, almost universally, is defined as "fair value" or "fair market value." The techniques used by appraiser and assessor alike are those in common use for other appraisal purposes.

FIGURE 3.2 "Estate Freezing"

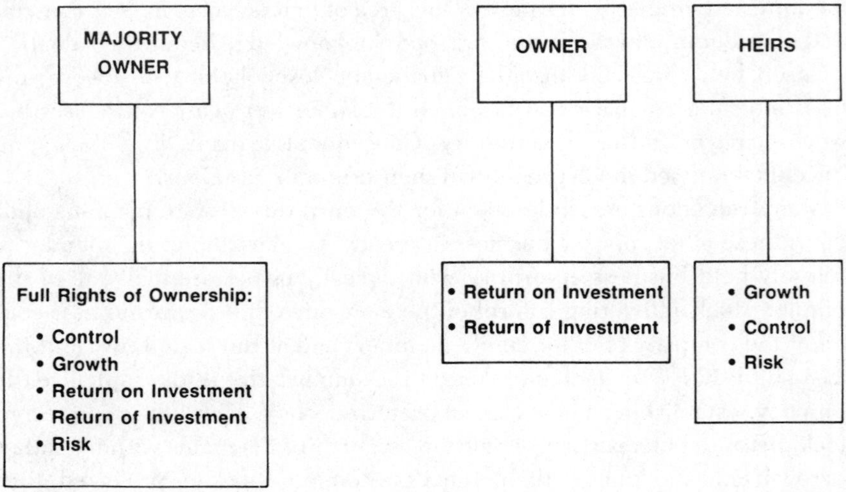

FIGURE 3.3   Recapitalization

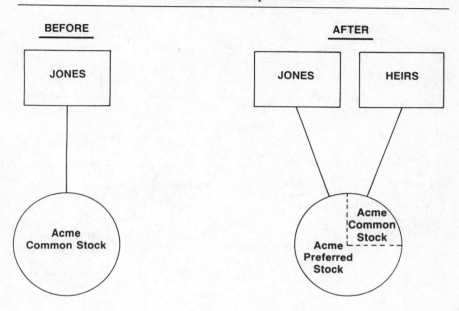

Most often, valuation disputes between taxpayer and taxing authority arise with regard to commercial and industrial properties that are unusual or unique facilities. By that is meant properties that are very large, or are suited for limited uses. Examples would include a manufacturing plant covering thousands of acres, a coal unloading facility beside a navigable river, a section of a cross-country pipeline, or a utility power plant. The valuation of such properties can be a complex endeavor, since the market for such properties is not as active as for residential real estate. In addition, the value of such property is closely linked to the economics of the business to which it is dedicated, because such properties are not easily converted to other uses. In subsequent sections are discussed the valuation techniques that are suited for this situation.

Another common property tax issue arises when a business is acquired. The purchase price of the enterprise may be equated, by the assessing authority, to the value of the physical properties of the business. It is then necessary for the taxpayer to demonstrate that the enterprise value includes such assets as working capital and intangible assets that are typically not subject to property taxes.

FIGURE 3.4   Holding Company Reorganization

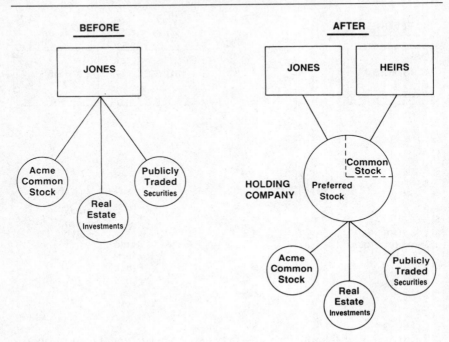

Corporate Reorganization

The disproportionate reduction in individual tax rates as a result of TRA is expected by some to encourage owners of corporations to change to the Subchapter S form of corporation, in which profits are taxed at the individual level. Perhaps in anticipation of this, TRA also tightened some of the provisions pertaining to such a conversion.

An S corporation, selling or distributing property within a period of 10 years after conversion, will have to segregate the amount of gain resulting from appreciation *before* conversion from that which occurred *after*. An independent appraisal of assets at the time of conversion to S status would accomplish this segregation of value.

Another new provision of TRA is a series of severe limitations on carryovers of net operating losses (NOL) and other credits. The primary thrust is to limit NOL carryforwards as part of acquisitions. The taxable income that can be offset by an NOL after a change in ownership is limited to an amount calculated by multiplying the *fair market value* of the corporation's stock by

FIGURE 3.5   Partnership Reorganization

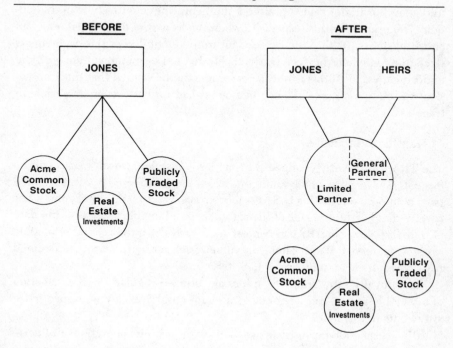

the federal long-term tax-exempt rate (to be published by the Department of the Treasury).

There are complex rules governing that which constitutes an applicable change of ownership, but this is a new situation in which value enters into the tax law.

Trademark Transfers

Section 1253 of the IRC provides that a franchise, trademark, or tradename may be transferred and not treated as the sale of a capital asset if the transferor retains significant power, rights, or continuing interest in the property. The transaction becomes similar to a "lease" of the property, with payments usually made over some agreed-upon period and which may or may not be contingent on use or sales levels. The payments are deductible by the transferee as a trade or business expense.

In most cases, many taxpayer-transferees prefer to have the franchise, trademark, or tradename appraised before entering into this type of transaction. The reason for this (especially when this is part of the acquisition of an entire business), is that the case for future deductibility of the payments is strengthened when they can be demonstrated to be commensurate with the underlying value. If this is not the case, it could be argued that this transaction was simply a tax avoidance tactic and had no basis as an arm's-length transaction.

Transfer of Intangibles

The TRA significantly changed the standards by which royalty rates will be evaluated in cases in which intangible assets are transferred between related parties into or out of the U.S. Formerly, taxpayers could determine a fair royalty rate for the transfer of the rights to an intangible asset as of the date of transfer. Now, the IRS can contest such a royalty if the related intangible asset is deemed to have gained in value. Such an increase in the deemed royalty results in an increase of U.S. tax.

Since royalty rates and license fees are utilized regularly in the valuation of intangible assets, some appraisers and appraisal firms are equipped to assist clients in this field.

IRC Section 936 permits corporations with business operations in Puerto Rico and other U.S. possessions to realize a tax credit on possession-source income. Part of this income is to be paid or allocated to a U.S.-related party according to either a cost-sharing or a profit-split method. Part of the cost-sharing formula is a measurement of an arm's-length royalty based on the current income stream attributable to the intangible. Again, this is an area in which a professional valuation specialist can be of assistance.

FINANCING

Collateral

The value of property is often the foundation for debt and debt-like financing, such as:

1. *Mortgage bonds* are secured by claims on specific assets of the issuer so that, in the event of default, the bondholder has a claim on the assets or the proceeds from their liquidation.

2. *Mortgage loans* are typically secured by real estate on which the mortgage holder has first claim in the event of default.

3. *Other debt* financing often requires a security interest in assets, such as inventories, accounts receivable, leases, or royalty and license income.

An appraisal is an integral part of financing arrangements, especially where specific property is to be collateral.

The quality of real estate appraisals has recently been the subject of concern in financial institutions, federal and state government agencies, and in the legislature. Defaults of financial institutions have revealed that loan commitments have exceeded the value of the property secured. It is not always clear whether this is the result of an over-optimistic appraisal or an over-aggressive lending institution, but it is a subject for legitimate concern. The safety net of inflation has been removed, for the time being, and rapidly escalating real estate prices no longer cover up bad appraisals and bad loans, whatever their cause.

Appraisals for financing purposes represent considerable exposure for the appraiser and extra caution is warranted. As will be discussed in a later chapter, there are material differences in the types of value (*premises* of value), and it is imperative that there be a clear understanding between appraiser and lender as to the assumptions to be considered on a given assignment.

Consider a Douglas DC-6, sans wingtips, parked on a downtown site and used as an operating restaurant. The one-time aircraft no doubt has value and was worth the investment to modify, move, and install. What would be the value to a mortgage lender, however, if the business fails?

Fairness Opinions

A proxy statement issued in connection with the purchase of a corporation's shares or a "tender offer," in which an acquirer publicly announces an offer to exchange cash or stock for the stock of a target company, often contains a fairness opinion. A fairness opinion is provided by an appraiser or other financial advisor, and is usually in the form of a letter report that is appended to the document. Such a letter would take the following general form:

Board of Directors
ABC Company
Philadelphia, Pa.

Dear Sirs:

You have requested our opinion as to the fairness, from a financial point of view, to ABC Company ("ABC") and its shareholders of the terms of the Purchase Agreement between ABC and XYZ Company ("Buyer").

We have acted as financial advisor to ABC with respect to the proposed transaction. In forming our opinion we have (1) reviewed the information contained in the Proxy Statement, including the historical financial statements and business information on ABC, (2) reviewed certain other public information regarding ABC, (3) participated in discussions with the management of ABC regarding its business and prospects, (4) reviewed the reported historical stock prices and trading volume of the common stock of ABC, (5) reviewed published financial and securities information of certain other publicly traded companies, (6) reviewed various financial aspects of other recent buyouts and business combinations, and (7) conducted such other financial studies and analyses of the foregoing information as we deemed appropriate.

In rendering this opinion, we have relied without verification or investigation on the accuracy, completeness, and fairness of all financial or other information provided to us. We did not review ABC's corporate charter, minute books of directors or shareholder meetings, pending litigation, nor did we make inquiries of customers, suppliers, competitors, general creditors, regulatory bodies, or others. Our opinion is based upon general economic, business, market and monetary conditions and prospects of the company existing and known to us on the date hereof.

Based upon and subject to the foregoing, it is our opinion that the amount of $18.45 per common share to be received by ABC shareholders is fair to ABC and its shareholders from a financial point of view.

LITIGATION

A number of appraisal situations are associated with litigation, either because they are always the subject of a court action or regulatory hearing or because they usually require adjudication.

On an assignment in which litigation is probable, a client should inquire into the experience of an appraiser as an expert witness. It may be appropriate to have one's attorney request other attorney references where previous engagements have gone forward to litigation. Not all appraisers, however technically competent, are good expert witnesses, and being a "good" expert witness is not the same in each and every case. Some cases are emotional and combative; others require very strong credentials or the ability to explain a complex subject to a jury in a patient and effective manner.

Condemnation

Governmental units, public authorities, and quasi-public entities such as public utilities have the right to take privately owned real estate for public use under the right of eminent domain. In the U.S, this is called *condemnation*, in Canada, *expropriation*. Such a taking is to be justly compensated. The determination of "just compensation" leads often to litigation.

Where the taking is of an entire parcel of property, just compensation is defined as the fair market value of the property. Where the taking is of only a portion of the property, just compensation may comprise the value of the part taken *plus* the reduction in value of the remaining part because of the taking.

Condemnation valuations can be complex, especially when they involve partial takings and consequential damages, and a party to such a proceeding would be well advised to retain an appraiser who is experienced in this area and in the jurisdiction where possible litigation will take place.

Distribution of Marital Property

An appraisal assignment for the purpose of dividing marital property may involve a myriad of assets and asset rights:

1. Real estate.
2. Lessors interest.
3. Easement interest.
4. Business enterprise.
5. Capital stock.
6. Securities.
7. Pension interest.
8. Personal injury award.
9. Litigation interest.
10. Intellectual property.
11. Professional degrees and licenses.

12. Personal property.

13. Collections (fine arts, antiques, etc.).

The valuation methodology in these cases is the same as for other litigated matters, but it is advisable to retain the services of an appraiser experienced with the specific property at issue and experienced in the jurisdiction, since state laws vary considerably.

Regulatory Proceedings

In years past, valuations were very much a part of rate regulation. Utilities, and other regulated entities, were permitted rates that would provide the opportunity to earn a fair return on the *fair value* of property devoted to public service. The Supreme Court of the United States in *Smyth v. Ames* said:

> We hold, however, that the basis of all calculations as to the reasonableness of rates to be charged by a corporation maintaining a highway under legislative sanction must be the fair value of the property being used by it for the convenience of the public. And in order to ascertain that value, the original cost of construction, the amount expended in permanent improvements, the amount and market value of its bonds and stock, the present as compared with the original cost of construction, the probable earning capacity of the property under particular rates prescribed by statute, and the sum required to meet operating expenses, are all matters for consideration, and are to be given such weight as may be just and right in each case. We do not say that there may not be other matters to be regarded in estimating the value of the property. What the company is entitled to ask is a fair return on the value of that which it employs for the public convenience.[3]

In recent years, most regulatory jurisdictions, even those in which "fair value ratemaking" is still the law, have equated original cost (or net book value in the case of plant-in-service) to fair value, and therefore appraisals of property are no longer an integral part of a utility rate proceeding.

It should be recognized, however, that many of the methods for valuing property other than real estate came from engineering studies performed in support of utility rate cases. More important, the techniques developed to analyze the service life of property to establish utility depreciation rates are still the foundation of economic life studies for all kinds of property.

Most valuations for rate proceedings are performed by appraisers who are specialists. Utility property, by its very nature, is special-purpose property with unique characteristics that must be properly considered in a valuation, and the regulatory environment is a unique business atmosphere that also has an effect on value.

Damages

Litigation involving damages to property, a business enterprise, or intangible assets may require the services of an appraiser. Property damage matters, from the valuation perspective, are very similar to casualty loss situations discussed previously under taxation. The same principles would apply to a business enterprise, that is, the value before the event as compared to the value after. For example, in assessing the damage to a business resulting from the theft of customer information by a competitor, the earning power of the enterprise before and after the loss would be measured.

Damage to intellectual property can be more difficult to assess. For example, a very specialized mailing list owned by a charitable organization is loaned to a company for the purpose of charitable solicitation. That company also uses the list for other, unauthorized solicitations which "over-use" the list, rendering it less effective to the original owner.

Shareholder Rights

A majority of shareholders can effect the merger, consolidation, or sale of assets of a corporation. A majority for this purpose is defined by corporate charter or state law. Minority shareholders cannot block such an action, but if they believe the transaction is unfair, their remedy is through the exercise of their right of appraisal:

> Dissenting minority shareholders derive their appraisal rights under statutory authority. . . . Statutes authorizing appraisal rights were instituted to protect dissenting minority shareholders from decisions of majority shareholders that altered the nature of their original investment. Once the minority shareholder has completed the necessary requirements to effect the appraisal, he or she must take the appraised value of stock and relinquish his or her share holdings.[4]

The appraisal standards to be applied in shareholder disputes are those previously discussed under estate and gift tax matters. In most cases, this situation arises in connection with closely held stock and the provisions of Revenue Ruling 59-60 are of prime consideration.

62 WHEN VALUATION SERVICES ARE NEEDED

MANAGEMENT

In a number of situations an appraisal is commissioned as an aid to management decisions or to form the basis for agreements between companies and other companies, employees, or shareholders.

Joint Ventures

One form of joint venture between two or more business entities or individuals involves contributed property rather than cash. As an example, a new corporation might be formed with one company contributing patents and manufacturing know-how and the other contributing physical plant and an assembled workforce. Each contributor might receive common stock in the new company in proportion to the value of property contributed.

The proportionate share of the venture would determine future profit (or loss) sharing as well as the cost basis on which future gains or losses would be calculated in the event of a sale of the enterprise.

The permutations are endless, but most joint ventures have some appraisal requirement.

Purchase and Sale

One of the most common appraisal situations is the valuation of property for management prior to its sale or purchase. This can include:

1. Individual assets, such as a plant site, real estate, used equipment, a license, a patent, or a trademark.
2. A business enterprise being considered for purchase.
3. A division or subsidiary being considered for sale.

The board of directors of a corporation may have to evaluate tender offers received or proposals to acquire other corporations. In each case, they have a fiduciary responsibility to shareholders. Increasingly, directors obtain the services of outside experts, appraisers included, to assist them in their decisions as to what to recommend to shareholders.

It is important to note a distinction between an appraisal and a consultation performed for a potential buyer or seller of property:

An appraisal is an estimate of the price that a willing buyer and seller would agree upon after negotiation and represents an amount that is fair to both.

A *consultation* for a potential buyer or seller, although it might *include* an appraisal as defined above, might also provide a *range* of values and might consider *specific* buyers and sellers, alternate uses of the property, payment alternatives, or negotiating positions.

An *appraisal* seeks market value, which has been defined as the "most probable buy-sell price."[5] It seeks the value of a share of stock which is quoted as "$9.50 bid, $11.00 ask." A *consultation* seeks to provide guidance to the "bidder" or "asker."

Employee/Stockholder Agreements

Several contractual arrangements between a company and its employees and/or stockholders may be based on appraised values. These usually are in connection with the purchase of stock in the company, and most often are required in closely held corporations.

A founder/entrepreneur usually desires to retain control over a company even though it may be necessary to sell some common stock to obtain needed financing or to attract employees with special skills or experience. One vehicle for this is to have agreements with such stockholders that provide the company with the right of first refusal on the sale of such stock and/or the termination of employment or death of the employee or stockholder. Such agreements usually have some provision that addresses the price at which an exchange will take place.

Some agreements have a formula for calculating the exchange price. A formula may by simple, such as "120% of book value of common equity at the most recent year-end," or may be very complex. It is quite difficult to develop a formula that will end up being fair at the time it is called upon. This is especially true of emerging high technology or service businesses in which this situation is most likely to arise, since in this type of business it is essential to attract highly qualified people whose technical skills often are more advanced than their business experience.

A more serviceable technique is to specify a value determined by a qualified business appraiser. In the event that the parties cannot agree, each can retain an appraiser, and if no agreement is reached then, the appraisers select a mutually agreeable third appraiser whose arbitration is binding. Although this technique appears to leave more "to chance," it has a better opportunity of achieving an equitable result.

REFERENCES

1. Financial Accounting Standards Board. *Accounting for Leases*. FASB Statement No. 13, Stamford, CT, 1980.

2. *Ibid*.

3. Anson Marston, Robley Winfrey, and Jean C. Hempstead, *Engineering Valuation and Depreciation*. Ames: Iowa State University Press, 1953, p. 20.

4. Marc J. Lane, *Purchase and Sale of Small Businesses*. New York: Wiley, 1985, pp. 398–399.

5. Henry A. Babcock, *Appraisal Principles and Procedures*. Washington, DC: American Society of Appraisers, 1980, p. 117.

4

BASIC VALUATION PRINCIPLES

To understand the appraisal process, it is necessary to review some of the underlying principles touched upon in earlier sections. In the context of providing specifications to the appraiser and evaluating proposals for service, the importance of the *premise of value*, the use of different *valuation methods*, and the concept of *depreciation* were noted. A basic understanding of these three subjects will greatly assist in communicating with an appraiser and in evaluating an appraisal product.

PREMISE OF VALUE

Babcock[1] describes *value* as ". . . expressible in terms of a single lump sum of money considered as payable or expended at a particular point in time for property, i.e., the right to receive future benefits beginning as at the particular time-point." *Value* is not the same as *price* or *cost*, though at times they are equivalent. When we speak of "getting a bargain" or "paying dearly" for something, we recognize the difference between price and value. Oscar Wilde described a cynic as, "A man who knows the price of everything and the value of nothing,"[2] again underlining this distinction.

Since value is represented by all future benefits of ownership compressed into a single payment, value is continually changing as those future benefits increase or decrease with the passage of time. Therefore an opinion of value can only be expressed relative to a given moment. Every appraisal has, then, as "as-of" date and the value opinion expressed therein is meaningful only at that time.

The future benefits of ownership can also not be quantified without defining *whose* ownership is assumed and/or the underlying *purpose* of the appraisal.

This is the most essential specification in the entire appraisal process and also one that is poorly understood by appraisal clients and that often leads to misunderstandings and even litigation. An appraisal assignment cannot proceed without a definitive premise of value. One cannot simply ask, "What is my car worth?" Value does not exist in the abstract and must be addressed within the context of time, place, potential owners, and potential uses. If value "is in the eye of the beholder," we need to know who the "beholder" will be: an insurance company; a used-car dealer; a neighbor; a tax assessor; an accountant; the executor of an estate; or a dealer in scrap metal.

Sometimes identifying the recipient of the appraisal will also define the value premise, since the requirement of certain users has been defined by custom. In other cases, it is necessary to determine how the appraisal will be used:

1. To estimate the cost of replacing property.
2. To determine insurance coverage.
3. To assist in setting a selling price.
4. To set the amount of a charitable donation.
5. To calculate the amount of estate, gift, or income taxes.
6. To determine the amount of a damage claim.
7. To estimate the value of property as collateral in a loan transaction.
8. To estimate the price a property would bring at auction.

Each appraisal use and purpose has a specific premise of value that is appropriate.

A careful definition of value is most important in appraisals of certain types of property. The more that a property is designed, constructed, or suited for a special purpose, the more difference there will be in value measured by different premises. Few properties are more specialized than America's Cup yachts. Constructed to rigid specifications and subject to continual change as technology, materials, and designs improve, the yachts are suited for little besides "around the buoys" racing, and require a large and highly trained crew to operate. Their reproduction or replacement cost is tremendous, yet their market value after the series of races approaches scrap value very quickly (especially for a losing boat).

At the other extreme, if one were called upon to appraise a new twenty-dollar bill, the premise of value would be immaterial to the result. It would not matter *who* the appraisal was for, or for what *purpose*, or at what *time* (assuming the conclusion were to be stated in terms of dollars, and not buying power). This property's complete liquidity negates the value differences that would result from assuming different value premises.

The paragraphs that follow introduce several definitions of value as well as several types of cost and indicate for each its most common usage by appraisers.

Cost of Reproduction

The cost as of the appraisal date to construct an *identical* property is known as cost of reproduction. For an 1850-vintage, New England textile mill building, this would be the cost of constructing an edifice with thick brick walls, wooden floors, high ceilings, small windows, and the like.

Cost of reproduction is useful:

1. To measure a partial loss for insurance purposes, since it is assumed the damaged property will be restored in keeping with the whole.
2. As a starting point to develop other measures of value.

Cost of Replacement

This is the cost, as of the appraisal date, that would be incurred to obtain a property with equivalent *utility* to the subject. For an 1850-style mill building, this would be a structure that provides the same floor area and amenities, but constructed to modern standards. The replacement cost of a steam-driven pump would be the price of an electric pump of the same capacity.

Cost of replacement is used:

1. To determine insurance coverage or to measure insurable losses.
2. In capital budgeting for facilities replacement or additions.
3. As a starting point in determining other measures of value.

In the insurance industry, the term "replacement cost" is not the same as cost of replacement described here but rather cost of reproduction, previously defined.

Cost of Reproduction/Replacement Less Depreciation

Another type of value is calculated by reducing either cost of reproduction or cost of replacement by an amount that reflects the loss in value because of physical deterioration and, in some cases, obsolescence.

This measure of value is in common use in the insurance industry and is often referred to as "actual cash value." In the insurance context, depreciation is almost always limited to that arising from physical deterioration, since the underlying purpose of insurance is to restore the insured to a position before the damage. Property that might generally be considered "obsolete" could be very useful in some businesses or for specific purposes and require replacement in kind. There have been, however, circumstances in which obsolescence has been recognized for insurance purposes, as the case of an abandoned school building destroyed by fire.

The term "sound value" is also used, most often in an insurance context, as a synonym for "actual cash value."

the appraiser uses this measure of value as:

1. A value conclusion when the appraisal is for insurance purposes.
2. An intermediate in the determination of other forms of value.

Original Cost

This is the cost typically recorded on the books of an enterprise at some previous time for the purchase, construction, or creation of an asset, and may be a combination of materials, labor, overhead, taxes, interest, and other costs. It represents the costs incurred by a specific party, at a particular time, and in accordance with particular conditions and is related to value only by coincidence, since the costs, even when incurred, may have been unusually high or low.

For an appraiser, original cost is useful as:

1. A *rough* guide to reproduction cost at an earlier time.
2. Part of the balance sheet of a business enterprise.
3. A starting point in the development of reproduction cost by the use of price trends.

Book Cost

Also referred to as book value or net book value, this refers to original cost reduced by accounting depreciation as carried on the books of a business. In order to distinguish between "accounting depreciation" and "appraisal depreciation," the term "capital recovery" is used for depreciation for accounting purposes.

Though many business people think of book cost as a form of value, it is not. Property accounting practices vary widely. In some cases property disposed of is not removed (retired) from the books, and in others, property that is fully depreciated is written off and disappears from the accounting records. Capital recovery practices also vary widely, and so methods and lives are not consistent from company to company. Though most managers would prefer not to admit it, capital recovery rates are sometimes changed to "manage" earnings per share. Therefore it is highly unlikely that "accounting" depreciation matches the decline in value over time and even if the original-cost starting point was representative of value at some previous moment, depreciated original cost is not likely to equal current value.

Net book value does have relevance to the appraiser in the valuation of regulated utility property, in that earnings permitted by a regulatory commission are a function of book cost.

Book cost is, except for the regulated environment, useful to the appraiser only as a very rough benchmark suitable for "order of magnitude" comparisons.

Tax Basis

This is the same as *book value* described above, except that the calculation of capital recovery is in accordance with tax requirements. Capital recovery is usually calculated by some form of accelerated method and the life is determined by legislation rather than actual service life.

Tax depreciation methods and lives have changed so often and so significantly over the years that tax basis is of no use as a measure of any form of value.

Fair Market Value

Fair market value is the most commonly used measure and, therefore, the most misunderstood. The terms "market value," "fair value," "true value," and "exchange value" are found in appraisal literature, the law, and in court cases. The general misunderstanding and "fuzziness" surrounding this value concept are in no small way related to its indefinite use by attorneys in contracts and by legislators in law, both situations leading to litigation which in turn involves more attorneys and expert witnesses and, in the end, a judge who interprets all their mis-interpretations.

In fairness, the appraisal profession must take some of the blame for this situation, for not having been quicker to reach internal agreement and for not working more effectively to educate the public. With that aside, below is given yet another attempt to clarify this concept.

First, fair market value (FMV) embodies the concept of an *exchange* of property. Further, it defines the *conditions* of that exchange. There are, therefore, different types of fair market value as those conditions change. All, however, proceed from some basic concepts:

Fair Market Value is the amount at which a property would exchange . . .

> *two persons come together for the purpose of exchanging property for money (since an appraisal is made in terms of money)*

between a willing buyer and a willing seller . . .

> *these two persons* want *to make the exchange.*

neither being under compulsion . . .

> *neither of the parties is forced, by the other or by circumstances, to make the transaction.*

each having full knowledge of all relevant facts . . .

> *both parties are aware of what is included in the sale, the condition of the property, its history and possible use, and liabilities against it.*

and with equity to both.

> *the exchange will be fair to both parties, neither gaining some advantage in negotiation or in the terms of the sale.*

This is the definition of fair market value in its purest form. Appraisers will at times introduce minor modifications, such as the words "*might* exchange" rather than "*would* exchange," since no one knows precisely the amount until after the appraisal. Another common substitution is "*reasonable* knowledge" for "*full* knowledge," presumably since no one ever has absolutely full knowledge of anything.

The definition of FMV, as shown above, is often amplified to accommodate different types of property or different exchange conditions.

Property. Certain kinds of property, such as the twenty-dollar bill, need no amplification of the FMV definition, because it is a most single-purpose property whose use is clear.

Land is always appraised at FMV, and often the pure definition is used, because it is customary to assume that knowledgeable parties know the permitted uses of the subject land and the use that will yield the highest economic return. Under this assumption, the appraiser forms an opinion of the "highest and best use" of the land and bases the analysis on that, irrespective of how it is being used at the time. No knowledgeable buyer would purchase waterfront property in Atlantic City, New Jersey, for the purpose of farming, and the appraiser of such land does not have to define FMV in such a way as to avoid a potential misunderstanding. The appraiser's statement of opinion regarding the highest and best use removes any doubt about the basis of the conclusion.

The potential uses and value assumptions relative to a highly specialized property, such as a 12-meter yacht, have a great impact on value and are not nearly so susceptible to general agreement; therefore the value premise itself must be more specific. One common way of doing this is to add the phrase:

> . . . and assuming that the property will continue in its present use (or in continued operation).

This might apply to a yacht recognized to be a contender and assumes *continued use* in the purpose for which it was designed and built. Without this specification, an appraisal of the yacht might be very misleading.

Exchange Conditions. There are times when an appraisal should reflect the fact that there are unwilling buyers and/or sellers or that there is an element of compulsion present or that property being used for one purpose by the seller is purchased by the buyer for another purpose. These conditions introduce further modifications to the definition.

Continuing the example of the 12-meter yacht and assuming that it never won a race, it might be exchanged under various circumstances, all of which could be defined as some form of liquidation. By this is meant that the present owner wishes to convert the property into money because the property is no longer useful in its present role or capable of earning an adequate return as an investment. As used by appraisers, the term "liquidation" also connotes some form of compulsion on the part of the owner (seller), perhaps because the financial return on the property has not met expectations or because there are other, better opportunities for investment. The speed with which the seller hopes to achieve liquidity is a key value factor.

Orderly Liquidation. A situation in which there is a "reasonable" time in which to accomplish the sale. What is reasonable can vary considerably, depending on the type of property. The yacht is very special, probably high-priced, even under these circumstances, and has an appeal to a very small market. It might take six months to a year to advertise, engage brokers, and locate someone in the world with enough interest, money, and able-bodied relatives and friends to strike a deal.

Another buyer might purchase with the intent of an alternate use, such as a floating restaurant or training vessel. The exchange price would certainly be lower than for continued use because the buyer would consider the renovation costs or the cost of a more ordinary boat that could provide the same service.

A steel mill or petrochemical plant might require several years of worldwide marketing effort, and substantial conversion costs to achieve the same objective.

Forced Liquidation. The same transaction carried out more quickly, even at some sacrifice in selling price. Often this means selling to an intermediary such as a real estate developer or other dealer who buys with the intent of "repackaging" the property and reselling it at a profit. The exchange price would be further reduced by the dealer's holding costs and return on investment.

Auction. This circumstance is likely to result in the lowest exchange price since there is no particular effort to contact the best possible buyer prospects and since the objective is to dispose of the property "now." Auctions of machinery and equipment, store fixtures, and so on are usually on an "as-is, where-is" basis so that the buyer also considers the cost to remove and transport the property.

Conclusion. Fair market value has a number of permutations. In its purest form it represents an exchange between knowledgeable persons who are not coerced in any way. It can also refer to situations in which one of the parties is under pressure to complete the transaction or in which the time available for its completion is limited. The fair market value of business property is inextricably linked to its earning capability.

VALUATION TECHNIQUES

In as much as value can be defined as the present value of future benefits, a valuation needs only to *quantify* the future benefits and then *calculate* their present value. These future benefits may be in the form of income, as in the case of a security or investment real estate; services, such as the production of goods by process equipment or manufacturing machinery; use, such as mineral reserves or residential occupancy; or enjoyment, as in the case of fine arts or jewelry.

For property dedicated to a business enterprise, future benefits are preferably measured in terms of income. There are, however, instances in which an alternative measurement of future service is relied upon, as discussed below.

This discussion of valuation methodologies includes an explanation of appraisal depreciation as it pertains to value. A previous section pointed out the distinction between appraisal depreciation and capital recovery used in accounting. Separation of depreciation from valuation is difficult, since any attempt to measure future benefits of property ownership carries with it the necessity to quantify how long those benefits are going to last and how much time must pass before they are to be realized. In addition, one must consider how those benefits will be received, i.e., will they be great in the early years and then diminish (or vice-versa) or will they be equal each year?

Those who write about the appraisal process often present the subject as if the calculation of value can be made as one step, with depreciation to follow. Since, in fact, appraisers do not segregate these steps, it is not done here, even though it may make the explanation more complex.

There are three accepted valuation methodologies: cost, income, and market techniques. Other methods appear in texts, but some analysis will reveal that other methods are really forms of these three.

Cost Approach

The cost approach seeks to measure the future benefits of ownership by quantifying the amount of money that would be required to replace the future service capability to the subject property. This was defined above as cost of replacement. The assumption underlying this approach is that the *price* of new property is commensurate with the economic value of the service that the property can provide during its life. The marketplace is the test of this equation. If, for example, the price of a new machine were set at a level far above the present value of the future economic benefits of owning the machine, then none would be sold. If the opposite were true, then demand would outstrip supply and presumably the price would rise. The price of a new machine, absent some market aberration, is therefore equal to its fair market value.

Depreciation. The appraiser is rarely called upon to render an opinion of value on brand-new property, however, and the use of the cost approach nearly always brings with it the complexity of quantifying the reduction from ("brand-new") value due to the action of depreciation.

Figure 4.1 illustrates this concept. The future service to be provided by the property is represented by the area under the curve to the right of the measurement point. Thus, at the beginning of the property's life, the area under the entire curve represents future service, and value can be described as 100 percent or equal to cost. As one moves to the right along the time abscissa to point B, the area to the right of the measurement point (represented by the shaded area) is reduced. This reduction occurs not just because of the passage of time, of course, but because of all the factors that contribute to loss in value.

Assuming that the shaded and unshaded areas are equal, B represents the point at which one-half of the total (when new) *service capacity* has been exhausted. That point is not necessarily the point at which one-half of the *life* has been used (A represents age and C represents remaining life).

This decline in value begins to take place from the moment property is placed in service and results from:

1. Physical wear and tear which, for production machinery as an example, renders it increasingly unable to perform with the speed, dependability, and accuracy of a new counterpart.
2. Advancing technology which brings more capable, lower-priced, or more efficient machines to the marketplace.

These definitions of physical deterioration and functional obsolescence are sometimes referred to as *physical* and *functional depreciation*, and (along with their partner, economic obsolescence) could be called the "Big Three" in appraisal depreciation.

The *speed and pattern* of this decline in value can vary considerably, as can the relative importance of the two factors noted above. The following examples may serve to illustrate:

> A stapler would be expected to have a relatively long life, with little physical deterioration up to the time it is broken. Since stapling technology is not expected to change significantly, a loss in value from functional obsolescence would not be rapid. The availability of low-cost staplers on the market could have some effect, since the value of a stapler at a point in time cannot exceed the cost of a new replacement. The pattern of decline in value would look something like Figure 4.2.

FIGURE 4.1 Depreciation Concepts

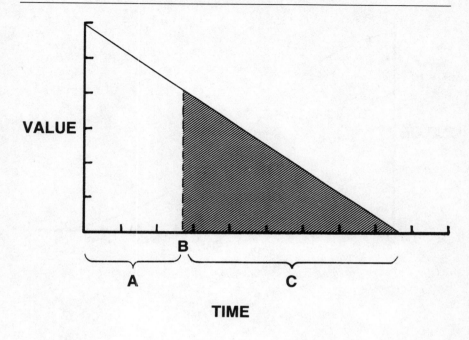

VALUE

B

A

C

TIME

FIGURE 4.2 Depreciation—Primarily Physical

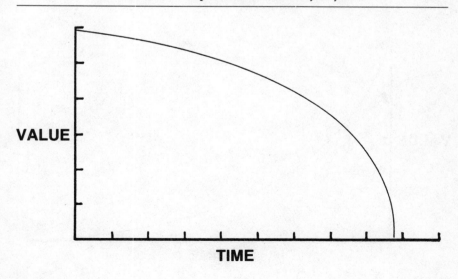

VALUE

TIME

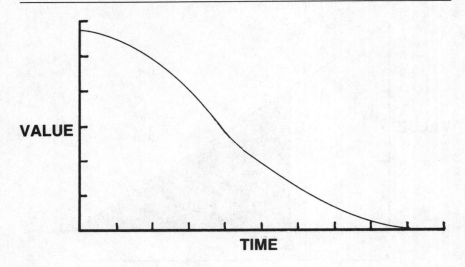

FIGURE 4.3   Depreciation—Physical and Functional

VALUE

TIME

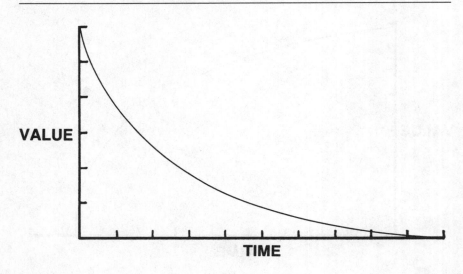

FIGURE 4.4   Depreciation—Primarily Functional

VALUE

TIME

A pump, on the other hand, would be expected to deteriorate in value according to its physical condition and due to factors of functional obsolescence and the pattern might appear as in Figure 4.3. This is a typical pattern observed in studies of the service life of physical property.

A personal computer would be the reverse of the pump, with physical deterioration being much slower than functional obsolescence caused by advances in technology, which would be rapid and controlling with respect to value. Its decline in value would be sharp in the early years, as illustrated by Figure 4.4.

Cost-approach valuation usually begins *either* with a determination of the current (as of the appraisal date) cost to obtain an unused replica of the subject property:

Cost of Reproduction New (CRN)

or the cost of obtaining a property of equivalent utility:

Cost of Replacement (COR)

When there is a difference between these two amounts, it is usually because COR represents a less-costly substitute, one element of functional obsolescence.

The next step is to reflect *physical depreciation*, since the subject is presumably not new. How much of the future service is gone because of wear and tear?

If the replica is not "state-of-the-art" or suffers from design or operating deficiencies that reduce its desirability when compared with similar properties available in the marketplace, then *functional obsolescence* must be reflected to obtain:

Replacement Cost Less Depreciation (CORLD)

Stated as a formula:

Cost of Reproduction New (CRN)
or
Cost of Replacement (COR)

> *Less:* Physical Depreciation
> *Less:* Functional Obsolescence
> *Equals:* Replacement Cost Less Depreciation (CORLD)

It is not always necessary to step through this progression if one can determine an intermediate value directly.

The last element necessary to determine fair market value by the cost approach is to reflect *economic obsolescence*, the third in the "Big Three" of depreciation factors. It is similar in concept to "highest and best use" as applied to real estate. This concept is based upon the assumption that property devoted to business use achieves full fair market value only when it is capable of contributing to the earnings of that business and when those earnings are capable of providing a reasonable rate of return on all the property devoted to the enterprise.

In other words, a new, state-of-the-art production line for hula hoops has a low fair market value because it is devoted to a business that is unlikely to earn a return adequate to justify an investment at a higher value. Thus the fair market value of assets in a business is dependent to some degree on factors that arise entirely outside of the particular circumstances of the individual asset. The fair market value of an asset can be significantly degraded by the economics of the business to which it is devoted. The extent to which it is degraded depends on the type of asset it is. Unique assets may suffer considerably, since they have little use outside of the particular business. Other assets of general use may only suffer in value to the extent of the costs that would be incurred to remove them from the business and transport and install them in a new business and location for use in a more profitable industry.

For example, assume the existence of a fast-food restaurant under three different scenarios. It is part of the successful, nationally known "Gordo's" chain and is owned by a franchisee:

1. The owner, is doing well in the business and, wishing to retire, desires to sell the property together with the franchise.

    Result—The owner is selling a going business with earnings that justify an investment by a purchaser equal to the current fair market value of the land and building as well as the franchise, goodwill, and other intangible assets. The fair market value might be $800,000.

2. The owner is making very little in this business and wants to liquidate in order to invest the proceeds elsewhere.

    Result—The owner is offering a marginal business. A potential buyer may feel that he or she could be successful by more efficient operation, or may convert the location to another type of fast-food operation. In this case, the buyer is interested in the physical property and does not consider intangible assets to have value. Such a buyer might also reduce the offer price by the costs of conversion to a new restaurant chain. The fair market value might be $500,000.

3. The owner is losing money and the location is no longer suitable for fast-food operation.

    Result—The owner must offer the location to an alternate user. The price would likely be the FMV of the land plus any value that might exist in the building for other uses. In an extreme case, the building might have no value or the value of the land might be reduced by the cost of removing the improvements in order to clear the land for other use. The fair market value might be $250,000.

The difference among these three scenarios is the earning power of the assets being offered for sale. The physical depreciation and functional obsolescence of the fixed assets is the same in each case. If businss property is incapable of earning a reasonable return on an investment at its presumed FMV in continued use, then the FMV will be based, at least in part, on a liquidation premise.

If the owner of a manufacturing plant is consistently unable to generate adequate earnings from the facility, then the investment would be liquidated and alternate investment opportunities sought. Examples of this are reported daily in the financial press in the form of plant closings or the sale of complete operating divisions. Thus we are continually reminded that the fair market value of a business and individual assets within that business is dependent on earning power.

The same situation exists with other forms of investment. An investor in the common stock of a company whose prospects are dimming sees that investment declining in value because of the market decisions of other investors in the stock. The fair market value of the equity in the business falls as a result. The same thing happens to the market value of a similar business whose stock is not traded, only there is no daily record of its demise. There is an indestructible link between the fair market value of business property and its earning power.

The equation started above can now be completed and the full course of the cost approach in determining fair market value described:

Cost of Reproduction New (CRN)

or

Cost of Replacement (COR)

Less: Physical Depreciation
Less: Functional Obsolescence
Equals: Replacement Cost Less Depreciation (CORLD)
Less: Economic Obsolescence
Equals: FAIR MARKET VALUE

In this formula, the appraiser begins with the cost of a new replica of the subject property and, after considering all forms of depreciation, ends with an indication of fair market value by the cost approach.

The cost approach is especially useful for appraising highly specialized property, such as a foundry, a reservoir, a steel mill, coal unloading facilities, a nuclear reactor, telephone switching centers, power plants, electric substations, or a satellite earth station.

The cost approach is also very useful as a valuation method for certain intangible assets such as computer software, an assembled workforce, or research and development programs. It is often used when other valuation methods are not applicable or to allocate values among assets that may have been valued in total by another means.

Income Approach

The income approach steps away from the cost of constructing or creating a new property to a consideration of the income-producing capability of the property. The underlying theory is that the value of property can be measured by the present worth of the net economic benefit (cash receipts less cash outlays) to be received over the life of the property.

The following discussion assumes that the reader is familiar with the "time value of money" and the concept that a dollar to be received in the future is worth less than a dollar to be received immediately. The term "present worth" refers to the current value of money to be received in the future and "discount rate" means the interest factor used in the present worth calculation. "Capitalization rate" will be used when the process involves a perpetual income stream.

The three essential ingredients of the income appraoch are:

1. The *amount* of an income stream.
2. An assumption as to the *duration* of the income stream.
3. An assumption as to the *risk* associated with the realization of the forecasted income.

These elements can be related to one another by means of a simple formula,

$$V = I/r$$

Where

V = Value of the earnings stream attributable to the property.

I = Income derived from employment of the property, representing the net of cash inflows and outflows.

r = Capitalization rate reflecting all the business, economic, and regulatory conditions affecting the risk associated with employing the property and achieving the prospective earnings.

For example, if an income of $100 will be received in perpetuity and the appropriate rate of capitalization is 10 percent, then the value of that income is:

$$\$100/.10 = \$1000$$

This is obviously the simplest of examples and one that never occurs in the appraiser's real life. Property ownership is rarely expected to produce income perpetually. Therefore the calculation is always more complex, and the determination of an appropriate capitalization rate is more complex as well.

Because business property is owned for the express purpose of earning a return on investment, the income approach is the strongest indicator of value for this type of property. There are, however, barriers between the appraiser and the universal application of the methodology. These barriers can only be overcome if the appraiser has a reasonable opportunity to establish clearly the three essential factors noted above.

A more complex, but still straightforward, example of an asset suitable for the application of the income approach is a contract with specific terms, such as a lease of real estate. Assume that the owner of real estate negotiates a lease of the property with the United States Postal Service (lessee). The lessee agrees to pay all expenses associated with the property and agrees to pay rent of $20,000 annually for 20 years. To the owner (lessor), this contract means an annual income of $20,000. Further assume that the lessor, after five years, decides to sell the lease contract in order to raise money for another investment. The real estate is not being offered for sale, only the lease. To a prospective buyer, the lease represents the right to receive an income of $20,000 per year for 15 years. What would be the fair market value of such a contract? The value is represented by the present worth of the income.

The amount of income is known ($20,000 per year). The duration of the income is known, (15 years). The risk of default on the rental payment is low, and so a low discount rate would be appropriate (say 10 percent). The present worth of $20,000 per year for 15 years at a discount rate of 10 percent is $152,122. An appraiser would conclude a fair market value of $150,000.

For an asset such as this, the income approach is absolutely the strongest indicator of value, since there is no reason to own this contract other than as an investment. In fact, this method incorporates the market approach, discussed below, in that the discount rate comes from an analysis of market rates of return for similar-risk investments. The conclusion, therefore, is representative of what other investors would calculate given the same facts and would be the market price if such contracts were offered to investors on a regular basis.

An additional complexity is introduced if the owner offered the real estate for sale, *subject* to the existing lease. In this case the prospective buyer would calculate the present worth of the lease income as above and then *add* the present worth of the value of the real estate fifteen years from now, when it came back into the owner's possession.

An appraiser is sometimes prevented from applying an income methodology because the three essential ingredients cannot be determined. A valuation of a taxicab in New York City might serve to illustrate. The taxi is operated by the owner for profit. Assume that the profit level is satisfactory to the owner, given the investment. The profit, however, arises from the interaction of several identifiable assets including the vehicle, the driver, the license to operate (medallion), and the company organization.

If the assignment is to value the vehicle, a 1986 Chevrolet, the income approach becomes difficult because the first step is to isolate the income produced by the car alone. A difficult undertaking at best. Here the appraiser would rely on a market approach (for the basic vehicle) and a cost approach (for painting, signs, meter, and so on).

The appraiser has a number of methods for estimating the *amount* of income that can be realized from the ownership of an asset and the appropriate discount rate (*risk* factor). These are discussed in Chapter 7. As to the expected *duration* of income, the appraiser again may be relying on a consideration of the three forms of depreciation. That is, the assets that are the source of the income may be subject to a decline both in value and in earning power. The income that they are capable of producing may decline proportionately, and this decline would become part of the calculation by the income approach.

The income approach is best suited for the appraisal of:

1. Contracts.
2. Licenses and royalty agreements.
3. Patents, trademarks, copyrights.
4. Franchises.
5. Securities.
6. Business enterprises.

The income approach indicates fair market value directly, without intermediate calculations involving the three forms of appraisal depreciation.

Market Approach

The market approach is the most direct and the most easily understood appraisal technique. It measures the present value of future benefits by obtaining a consensus of what others in the marketplace have judged it to be. There are two requisites: (1) an active, public market and (2) an exchange of comparable properties.

The residential real estate market is a good example where these conditions are typically present. There is usually some activity in this market in a given area, and selling, asking, and exchange prices are public. Of course, not all residential properties are similar but, given enough activity, reasonable comparisons can be made.

Where these optimal market conditions do not exist, this approach involves more judgment and may become a less reliable measure of value.

Active Market. The ideal situation is to have a number of property exchanges to use in this analysis. One sale does not make a market. There are, for example, publicly traded common stocks in which only a few shares are traded in a year. Their exchange price has much less validity as a measure of value than, say, General Motors stock in which thousands of shares are traded each day. All requisites are there except activity.

Public Market.   To be useful, the exchange consideration must be known or discoverable. The prices of common stock in the primary exchanges are known in minute detail. For other types of property, it becomes more difficult to discover the exchange price. Even with real estate, the published price may be misleading because of financing arrangements between buyer and seller that are not made public. Transactions between businesses, such as the sale of a plant, product line, or subsidiary, may be difficult or impossible to evaluate because competitive pressure motivates the participants to keep the details confidential.

Adjustments for Comparability.   The best of all worlds for an appraiser to find, for a subject property, an arm's-length sale of an exact replica property, across the street, the day before the appraisal. Unfortunately (or perhaps fortunately for appraisers) this does not happen with enough regularity to eliminate the need for adjustments when "comparable sales" are not exactly comparable. Real estate appraisers continually grapple with the problem of quantifying differences in property, so that the location, amenities, zoning, size, shape, and topography of comparable sales can be equated to the subject to provide an indication of value. Appraisers using this approach for other types of property have the same challenge, but comparability tends to be more obvious—one either has it or not—and there are fewer nuances.

Adjustments for Time.   Sometimes it is necessary to utilize sale information that is not contemporaneous with the appraisal. In this case the appraiser must adjust for price changes over time, and this may necessitate a separate study of changes in property value in the subject area during a recent period of time so as to develop some specialized indices to use in the adjustment process.

With this background, the reader can gain a picture of the strengths and weaknesses of the market approach. Where there is a good base of information about the sales of properties that are similar to the subject, the market approach can be the strongest indicator of value. As the number of "comparable sales," or information about them, dwindles, or when the lack of comparability makes adjustment speculative, this approach ceases to be useful.

The market approach is then most effective for:

1. Real estate.
2. Machinery and equipment in general use.
3. Vehicles.
4. General-purpose computer software.
5. Computer hardware.
6. Liquor licenses.
7. Franchises.

The market approach is very often useful in the valuation of capital stock or other types of securities or an entire business enterprise.
The market approach is typically least effective for:

1. Special-purpose machinery and equipment.
2. Most intangible assets.
3. Properties highly restricted by zoning, environmental restrictions, or other forms of regulation.

The market approach takes the appraiser right to the "bottom line" of fair market value. The assumption is that other buyers of comparable property were willing, had knowledge of all relevant facts, and struck a deal that was fair and, therefore, represented fair market value at that time and for that property. The market measures and adjusts for all forms of appraisal depreciation: physical, functional, and economic.

Summary

Cost, income, and market approaches are the appraiser's tools. Virtually any type of property can be valued using them. The appraiser should consider the use of all three for every property, because a comparison of the values resulting from each will either confirm the conclusions or highlight inconsistencies that should be investigated. This is not always possible, however, since it is obvious that some approaches are clearly not applicable in certain situations.

REFERENCES

1. Henry A. Babcock, *Appraisal Principles and Procedures*. Washington, DC: American Society of Appraisers, 1980, p. 95.
2. Oscar Wilde, *Lady Windermere's Fan*, Act III.

5

VALUING A BUSINESS

An appraiser views a business as an aggregation of assets, monetary, tangible and intangible. The term "business enterprise" is used for that package of assets and therefore the business enterprise value (BEV) is the value of that totality.

The *securities* of a business, which may be various forms of stock and debt, are, to the appraiser, quite separate and distinct. The valuation of the securities of a business can be very complex and a number of books address this subject alone.

VALUING A BUSINESS ENTERPRISE

Business Enterprise Defined

Every business enterprise, from a pushcart vendor of hotdogs to the largest multinational corporation, comprises three basic elements: working capital, tangible assets, and intangible assets, as shown in Figure 5.1.

Net Working Capital. Net working capital is defined as current assets less current liabilities. Current assets include:

Cash.

Short-term investments, such as marketable securities.

FIGURE 5.1   Three Basic Elements of a Business Enterprise

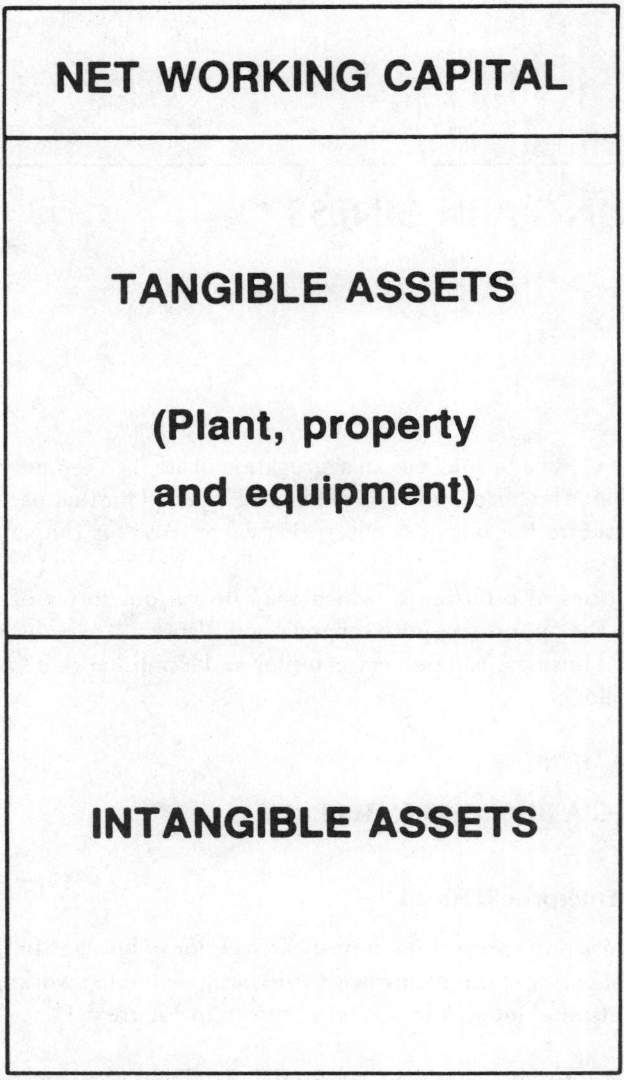

NET WORKING CAPITAL

TANGIBLE ASSETS

(Plant, property and equipment)

INTANGIBLE ASSETS

Receivables, from all sources, less reserves.

Inventories, including:

    Raw materials.

    Work in process.

    Finished goods.

Prepayments.

Current liabilities include:

Accounts payable.

Current portions of long-term debt.

Federal income taxes and other accrued items.

In most cases, current assets exceed current liabilities and net working capital is a positive amount. There are businesses, however, able to operate quite satisfactorily with an excess of current liabilities, or negative net working capital. These are usually businesses in which the customers pay in cash (such as a restaurant) or in advance for services rendered so there is no delay in collections.

Tangible Assets. Tangible assets are usually shown on the balance sheet as "Plant Property and Equipment." Included in this asset category would be land, buildings, machinery and equipment, office furniture and equipment, vehicles, construction in progress, and reserves (of natural resources).

Intangible Assets. Intangible assets usually do not appear on a company's balance sheet but are present in any case. This asset category might include an assembled workforce, trademarks and/or tradenames, contracts, patents, designs, customer lists, accounting and operating systems and records, supplier/distributor relationships, and goodwill.

Cost and Value. There have been several references to the balance sheet of a business and we will continue to use the balance sheet as a reference structure in describing valuation techniques. There is good reason for this relationship in that the balance sheet represents the summation of all the historical transactions of the business. As pointed out previously, the balance sheet does not record value, it records cost. Therefore, what is included or excluded on the balance sheet is not determinative for the appraiser.

Figure 5.2 illustrates a balance sheet as it appears to an appraiser. The items inside the solid lines are those typically recorded for accounting purposes. The dashed lines indicate how the reflection of fair market value might change this accounting record.

This representation shows the most common difference between a balance sheet of cost versus one of value—the addition of intangible assets whose increased value is reflected in added value of common equity. As presented below, all the assets of a business can be valued and those values may be either above or below their recorded cost. A balance sheet restated in terms of value would, therefore, not necessarily resemble what is shown in Figure 5.2.

Sum of Assets Technique

This balance sheet restatement approach is one way that a business enterprise can be valued. An appraiser would most likely call this the "sum of assets" technique. The assumption is that when each of the elements of working capital and tangible and intangible assets are individually valued, their sum represents the value of the enterprise. Recalling the previous chapter, the reader might relate this to the cost approach as applied to an entire business.

This approach is also analogous to the start-up of a business:

1.   The start-up entrepreneur first accumulates cash, in the form of either equity or debt.

2.   The cash is then converted to property or property rights. Typically this is the process of renting a place of business, purchasing store fixtures or manufacturing machinery, vehicles, and the like. At this time some inventory of raw materials or finished goods would be purchased.

3.   Some of the cash would then be used to purchase services in the form of advertising or to hire employees. Other expenditures are made to establish business relationships, such as with a bank, with accounting advisors, with an attorney to perform legal services and obtain the proper licenses, permits, and so on.

4.   At this point the elements of a going concern have been assembled and sales to customers can begin.

FIGURE 5.2   Balance Sheet as It Appears to an Appraiser

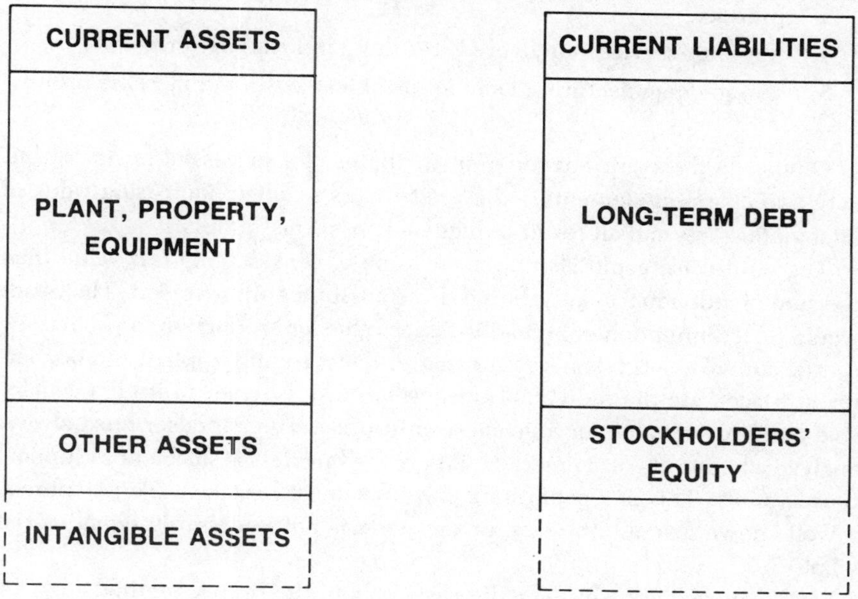

CURRENT ASSETS	CURRENT LIABILITIES
PLANT, PROPERTY, EQUIPMENT	LONG-TERM DEBT
OTHER ASSETS	STOCKHOLDERS' EQUITY
INTANGIBLE ASSETS	

5. When a satisfied customer returns or a new customer arrives on the recommendation of a previous one, patronage is established and goodwill comes into existence.

An appraisal of this start-up business would present some unique challenges. One logical method would be to appraise the individual assets—probably by a cost approach since they would have been so newly created. The indicated value would be comparable to the owner's investment if the purchases of goods and services were wisely made.

The sum of assets technique can be used for an established business as well. The appraiser might utilize the cost, market, or income approaches, as appropriate, for the individual assets that investigation shows are part of the business. The appraiser would then have to question whether the result indicated by this technique is an appropriate indicator of value for the enterprise. The value of the business could be *greater* than the sum of individual asset values if, for example:

1. The owner has chosen a superior location.
2. Competition is weak.

3. A large share of the market is captured with a new, patent-protected product.

4. Superior service is delivered, resulting in loyal patronage.

5. Unique manufacturing techniques reduce costs and increase profits.

Obviously these are not the only attributes of a successful business, but note two common elements—these attributes result in increasing value of intangible assets and all result in higher-than-normal profits.

The enterprise could also turn out to be of considerably *less* value than the sum of individual asset values if these attributes are reversed. The result would be a diminution of intangible asset value and reduction in profits.

The sum of assets technique, no matter how carefully applied and no matter how accurate the individual asset values are, is never in itself a conclusive indicator of value for a business enterprise. The appraiser must always analyze whether the earning capability of the business is sufficient to support those values. This is a confirming step that must be taken. To paraphrase a well-known axiom: "the sum of the parts is not necessarily equal to the whole."

You may well ask why, in a discussion about the proper methodology for valuing a business enterprise, begin with a technique that has so many shortcomings. Because this is where most non-appraisers begin: with a so-called cookbook approach. Take one real-estate appraisal, add to it an equipment valuation, fold in the inventory from the balance sheet, mix well with a pinch of customer list and a dash of goodwill, and presto—a business enterprise value. The variations are endless, but all proceed from the same, usually faulty, assumption.

Income Approach

The income approach, when applied to a business enterprise, begins with a projection of the income-producing *capability* of the business. It is based on the assumption that the value of the enterprise is dependent on the ability of all the assets to earn a reasonable return.

Figure 5.3 illustrates the interaction of the value of an enterprise, its earnings, and the value of its tangible and intangible assets:

At Point A—The business is losing money and, to avoid further loss, the owner would initiate the forced liquidation of fixed assets. Stated another

FIGURE 5.3   The Interaction Between the Value of an Enterprise, Its Earnings, and the Value of Its Tangible and Intangible Assets

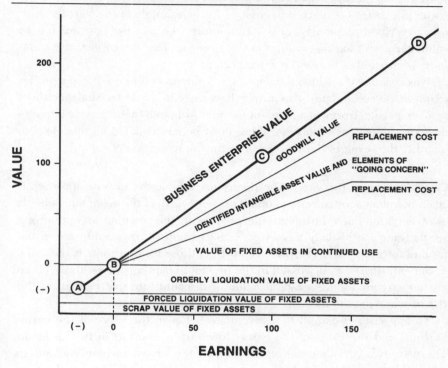

way, the assets should be deployed elsewhere in order to maximize their economic value.

At Point B—The business is breaking even and the owner therefore has the time to dispose of fixed assets in an orderly liquidation.

At Point C—The enterprise has adequate earnings and one would therefore expect to find a "full complement" of tangible and intangible assets, with no significant amount of economic obsolescence reflected in their value.

At Point D—The business is highly profitable, and tangible assets reflect value in continued use, to a maximum of their replacement cost, as do identifiable intangible assets. The enterprise has significant goodwill value, supported by its superior earnings.

Each of these situations presumes that earnings are stable at the level represented along the abscissa. The relationships are not precisely fixed when the earnings picture is expected to change. In the example of the start-up business described previously, one would not assume that the business has no value because it has no earnings of the moment. That is why earnings *capability* is stressed as the key, not actual earnings.

This is an area in which the appraiser is able to be more flexible than, for example, an accountant, who must reflect the enterprise on a balance sheet as a "snapshot," frozen at a moment in time. Although the appraiser is free to develop projections of income, there must be a calculation methodology to quantify the result of those projections into an indication of value.

Capitalization of Income. The theory underlying the income approach is again based on a measurement of the present worth of the economic benefits of ownership. For a business enterprise (with the seeming exception of a sports franchise or daily newspaper), the benefits of ownership are in the form of future profits. The present worth of those future profits is the value of the enterprise. As discussed in the previous chapter, one requires: (1) an income stream and (2) a capitalization or discount rate that recognizes the risk of achieving the income.

An appraiser is careful to differentiate between the value of the entire business and the value of the equity (ownership interest) in the business. There are two very different levels of income involved. Income available to pay for all types of capital, both debt and equity, is one. This is called return on investment (ROI). Income available to common shareholders is another and is called return on equity (ROE). Capitalizing ROI gives an indication of the value of the entire enterprise, whereas capitalizing ROE indicates the value of the equity interest only. The capitalization rates are also derived differently. The valuation of equity is addressed in a later section. The following discussion refers to the valuation of the entire business enterprise.

If the income is expected to be very stable over a long period of time, the valuation formula would be:

$$V = \frac{I}{R}$$

$$where \quad I = \text{income}$$
$$R = \text{capitalization rate}$$

If the income is expected to grow at a stable rate over a long period of time, the valuation formula would be:

$$V = \frac{I}{R - G}$$

Where   G = growth rate

Where the income is expected to grow erratically, or for a short period, then level off or continue at a stable rate, the valuation formula is expressed as the *sum* of the present worth of an income stream plus a reversion, defined as follows:

Present Worth of an Income Stream—the present value of the income expected to flow from the business during a finite future period. It is common to forecast income for three to five years into the future. Forecasts beyond that are unusual and most often used when there is a known life to a product because of contractual agreement or license or when a separate analysis of economic life supports a longer projection period.

Reversion—a business enterprise at the end of a near-term forecast still has value, since it is an ongoing entity. It is common to capitalize the income at the end of the forecast period into an indication of value at that time and discount the result to the present.

This is analogous to the situation of a landlord whose current real estate value is represented by the present worth of rental income plus the present worth of value of the property when it reverts at the end of the lease.

Expressed as a formula, this is:

$$V = \frac{I_1}{(1+R)^1} + \frac{I_2}{(1+R)^n} \cdots + \frac{V_n}{(1+R)^n}$$

where   Vn = value of the reversion

Adjustments to the Income Stream.   The first step in the income approach, when applied to a business enterprise, is to estimate the level of earnings that the enterprise is capable of producing in normal operations. This capability is not necessarily what the business is actually earning at the time of the appraisal. The appraiser may make adjustments to a current income statement that might include:

Income/Expense Item	*Adjustment*
Revenue	1. Increases to reflect new products or acquisitions or price increases.
	2. Decreases as products decline or market share is lost.
Cost of Goods	3. Adjustment for changes in inventory accounting method.
	4. Reductions in manufacturing costs as product matures.
	5. Changes due to supplier prices.
	6. Increases due to new labor contract.
Operating Expenses	7. Adjustment for excessive owner compensation.
	8. Adjustments for unusual research or development expenses.
	9. Adjustment of depreciation expense for new plant additions/retirements or new depreciation base of acquirer.
	10. Increases in selling expense for new product introduction.
Other Expenses	11. Adjustments to interest expense to reflect normal capital structure.
	12. Removal of income from non-operating assets.
Taxes	13. Adjustment to statutory rate when unusual deductions are shown.

In most cases, adjustments to revenues and expenses are minimal or, in the case of a publicly held corporation, may not be made at all. Adjustments of this kind are very often made when appraising a small, closely held business. The owner of such an enterprise is often not at all concerned with showing a profit on "the bottom line," desiring instead to minimize taxes. Owner's compensation is often in the form of a high salary, and not dividends, and there are often substantial "perks" in evidence. In another case, a business can be "squeezed" for every possible dollar of earnings in order to make it attractive for sale. Purchases of needed equipment or maintenance of existing machinery may have been deferred in order to enhance earnings.

These things would appear quite differently in a professionally managed, publicly held company. No value judgment is made about the relative skill or efficiencies of these two scenarios; it is just that the objectives are different.

Whether or not the financial statements are audited has no bearing on the need for this analysis. It is not the auditor's responsibility to determine an appropriate salary for the owner, the extent to which an owner's salaried relatives really work in the business, whether three Mercedes-Benz automobiles and a Florida condominium should be on the books, or whether equipment maintenance is properly done. This is not to say that the auditor doesn't know or have an opinion about these things, only that they are not now enumerated as part of financial statements.

The appraiser needs to know, however, what the business is capable of earning on a sustainable basis and cannot simply accept what the most current income statement shows. To many readers, this may seem presumptuous to the extreme on the appraiser's part. It is, however, no different from the way a real estate appraiser concludes the highest and best use of a property, *regardless* of how the present owner is utilizing it. It is also not an entirely capricious undertaking and the ground is nowhere near as "swampy" as one might think.

Certainly the owner of a business, whether a client or someone whose business is being purchased by a client, could, with a great deal of care and foresight, fabricate records and inspections and successfully mislead an appraiser or any other professional. In our opinion, attempts to do so are extremely rare.

Clients, however, are never completely indifferent to the outcome of an appraisal. Therefore, if an appraiser erroneously jumps to an optimistic conclusion (or pessimistic, depending on the client's bias), it is only natural that the client may not go out of his or her way to correct the situation.

The appraiser can follow several steps in order to obtain the information needed to make whatever adjustments are reasonable:

1. Inform the client at the outset that access will be needed to historical financial statements, contracts for supply and distribution, employee census data, leases, production records, historical sales by product line or item and by major customers, details of operating expenses that would show payroll expense by employee group, maintenance expenses, patent and trademark registrations, and the property rec-

ord detail supporting the plant property and equipment on the balance sheet.

2. Analyze the trends in sales and expenses and, if they are unusual, go into the detail to find out why.

3. Compare line items of revenue and expense with industry data from outside sources or from comparable or competitive companies.

4. Inspect company premises. This is very important, even if the assignment is to value the whole enterprise and not individual assets.

5. Obtain the services of specialists in real estate and/or machinery to evaluate rental rates, lease terms, equipment obsolescence and maintenance.

6. Obtain the client's permission to interview major customers, suppliers, or competitors.

It is not necessary to follow all of these steps in every case. Most appraisers begin with "gross" checks and, if these reveal anomalies, proceed with more and more detailed investigation until satisfied that an explanation is in hand.

In some ways, this process is more of an art than a science. The appraiser's experience is an important factor, both in the sense of overall business experience and specific experience within a certain industry. One's curiosity is aroused when certain members of the client management team are continually "unavailable" or when certain records cannot be located or do not exist. Most often, these situations are the result of well-meaning efforts and not an attempt at deception. The appraiser is shielded from some management member because "he is a real character and will talk your ear off about inconsequential things" or "she is such a pessimist you'll think we're going bankrupt tomorrow." Records are not produced because they are in such poor shape they are an embarrassment to the manager whose responsibility they are.

Answers to such questions as "Why did sales of that product fall last year?" or "Why is the raw material inventory so high?" may sound evasive. Every businessperson makes mistakes and none of us is anxious to reveal blunders, especially to an appraiser who is representing the company that just acquired ours.

A competent business appraiser will recognize these situations, be able to compensate for the apparent bias in the "interviewee," and be able to obtain the needed information without conducting interviews like the "Grand Inquisitor." A good appraiser is "people sensitive" and can provide assurance that an analysis and concern with trends is not to ferret out past errors but to gain an accurate picture of what is important to the business and its future.

This may appear to have been a digression, but it is important that the reader understand, from the appraiser's point of view, how one accumulates the facts upon which adjustments are made to a company's income statement.

Valuation requires an understanding of financial theory as well as sensitivity in dealing with people.

Calculation of the Income Stream. For the valuation of a business enterprise as defined here, most appraisers use *net cash flow* as the relevant income stream. Net cash flow is defined as:

> Earnings before interest and taxes
> *Less:* Income taxes at the statutory rate
> *Plus:* Depreciation and other non-cash expenses
> *Less:* Capital expenditures
> *Less:* Cash required to increase net working capital

The use of debt-free net cash flow eliminates the effect of how the business is presently financed and taxed (by substituting statutory tax rates) and also recognizes the future cash outlays that may be necessary to achieve the forecasted earnings. Net cash flow is calculated for the period of the forecast. When the reversion takes place, it is assumed that the net cash flow in the terminal year of the forecast will continue in perpetuity, with depreciation equal to capital needs so that further infusions of cash will not be necessary.

The underlying assumption at the reversion year is that product cycles or market share have matured and that future cash-flow growth is expected to be at a steady and sustainable rate.

Capital additions are estimated from specific plans for new plants to add capacity or new products, an analysis of present plant capacity, or more general indicators such as the historic ratio of plant investment per dollar of sales in the subject company or in the industry. Additions to net working capital are usually based on working capital turnover ratio analysis.

Rate of Return Determination. The appropriate rate of return to utilize in the capitalization of net cash flow is a weighted average cost of capital comprised of the after-tax cost of debt and equity. This is called by some the "band-of-investment" method. The components of this calculation are:

1. An appropriate capital structure, i.e., the relative proportions of debt and equity.
2. Cost of debt capital.
3. Cost of equity capital.
4. Income tax rate.

The most difficult components are the capital structure and the cost of equity capital. Both of these elements are typically obtained from analyses of companies in the same industry.

Capital structure determines the financial risk of the enterprise, with the amount of financial risk increasing as the amount of debt increases. Business risk (arising from the nature of the industry, competition, market share and volatility, and so on) is assumed to be balanced by financial risk. An enterprise with low business risk will be financed with more debt than one with greater business risk. Since debt capital costs less than equity capital, the owners of a business will be inclined to utilize as much debt as possible, consistent with the business risk of the enterprise. Therefore a comparison of the capital structure of similar (business-risk) companies is meaningful.

There are a number of techniques that appraisers use to estimate the cost of equity capital. These come from the field of security analysis and, while a complete discussion of the subject would go far beyond the scope of this book, some of the more common methods are described. These methods are based on the assumption that the cost rate for common equity is higher than that of debt because of the increased risk borne by the common stockholder in being "last in line" for the company's income. The common stockholder demands a premium to compensate for this added risk. Some refer to this as a "built-up" rate. Equity cost can then be expressed as:

$$R_e = R_{rf} + k$$

where R_e = cost of equity capital
R_{rf} = risk-free return, such as a long-term government bond yield to maturity
k = risk premium.

Risk premiums can range from 3 to 30 percent, depending on the relative risk associated with the achievement of the projected income stream. Some appraisers have developed categories of businesses according to their risk and have calculated ranges of premium for each category.

TABLE 5.1

Type of Capital	Capital Structure (%)	Capital Cost Rate (%)	Weighted
Debt	30	9.50	2.85
Equity	70	17.00	11.90
			14.75%

A more sophisticated technique for estimating the cost of equity capital is the Capital Asset Pricing Model (CAPM) which uses a broad stock market rate of return and a "beta" factor to quantify the risk premium:

$$R_e = R_{rf} + R_m - R_{rf})B$$

where R_m = return of the broad stock market.
B = beta factor, or the measure of the volatility of a stock's price versus the overall market.

A full calculation of equity cost rate using the CAPM is contained in Appendix A of the sample report in Chapter 10.

Whatever method used to arrive at an estimated equity cost rate, the overall cost of capital is calculated as shown in Table 5.1, using the other components of the rate of return.

On page 189 of the sample report in Chapter 10 is a calculation of a business-enterprise value by the income approach. In this case, the present worth of net cash flow has been calculated and added to the reversion to indicate a value of $21,739,000. The addition of a premium for control is a subject to be discussed later.

Market Approach

As noted in Chapter 4, the income and market approaches are not completely distinct from each other. The income approach described above uses data from the market to determine a rate of return and a capital structure. The market approach is based on an analysis of investor decisions which were most probably founded on an income capitalization.

To utilize a market approach in the valuation of a business enterprise, an appraiser would investigate and analyze the reported sales of other business enterprises. If s/he is extremely fortunate, one or two may be found and be similar enough to the subject to be of use. It becomes obvious that in order to be useful in the appraisal process, there has to be a high degree of comparability in the sales data or else the adjustment process becomes so extreme as to render the exercise worthless.

In recent years there has been a relatively active market for cable television systems. There is enough similarity in the tangible property and in the rates and operating expenses to make meaningful comparisons and to use this market data. The fair market value of a cable system is often expressed on a per-subscriber basis. This situation is, however, unsual and this direct market approach can seldom be used to value a business enterprise.

Figure 5.2 showed a balance sheet as it might be viewed by an appraiser. The "sum of assets" technique described thereafter addresses the value of the left side of that balance sheet. Since it is a *balance* sheet, the value of the enterprise might also be determined if one could value its right side. This is the so-called stock and bond, or stock and debt, technique. If the common equity of an enterprise can be valued, together with the liabilities of the business, an indication of BEV is obtained.

Usually the securities of a business are appraised individually for specific purposes, such as for a stockholder's estate, but the techniques are the same as one would use to value *all* of the securities of an enterprise and thereby the enterprise itself.

VALUING THE SECURITIES OF A BUSINESS ENTERPRISE

The securities of a business represent very specific interests. Each type of security has specific characteristics that affect value.

Long-Term Debt.   Debt securities typically include bonds, mortgages, or long-term notes. All are subject to various covenants or restrictions which might refer to interest rate, date(s) due, property used as collateral, sinking fund payments, restrictions on working capital or dividends, and whether additional debt can be issued.

The multiplicity and variety of these conditions can make valuation difficult; but in a simple form, debt securities are valued by calculating the present worth of the interest expense and principle repayments at a discount rate equal to that of similar risk debt at the time of the appraisal. Many homeowners made a similar calculation recently as home mortgage rates fell. The purpose was to determine whether the present worth of a new repayment schedule at a lower interest rate was sufficiently below the existing schedule (plus refinancing costs) to warrant the expense of refinancing.

Assume that an enterprise has debt on its balance sheet in the form of bonds. The face amount of the bond is recorded as long-term debt (i.e., $100,000) and the business pays interest annually at the rate of 12 percent ($12,000). In ten years, the bonds come due and the face amount must be returned to the bondholders. If the interest rate in the market for similar risk bonds as of the appraisal date is 10 percent, the value of the debt to the *bondholder* is $112,289 (the present value of $12,000 annual interest payment plus present value of the $100,000 reversion in 10 years, both at 10 percent market interest rate).

The value of these bonds to the *business* (debtor) is $87,711, because the same $100,000 of capital could be obtained for $10,000 annually, or $2,000 less. The company suffers an annual expense disadvantage of $2,000 which, discounted at 10 percent, equates to a negative $12,289. Stated another way, the business, were it not burdened with higher-than-otherwise interest expense, could earn an additional $2,000 annually. This, of course, ignores the tax implications for both bondholder and company, but illustrates the valuation principle.

Preferred Stock.   Preferred stock is a debt-like security that is valued similarly to bond debt. It is more difficult to locate comparable preferred stock trading in the market because, in addition to differences among issuing companies, there is a diversity in the rights attached to the security, such as:

1. Dividend rate.
2. Cumulative/non-cumulative dividend payment terms.
3. Voting rights.
4. Call provisions.
5. Convertibility (to other types of security).
6. Par value.
7. Preference in the event of corporate liquidation.
8. Participation in the receipt of earnings in excess of the stated dividend.

In addition to the specific terms of the preferred issue, one must consider the strength of the earnings that support the payment of dividends when selecting comparable issues. In general, the earnings available to pay for capital are first utilized for debt and then for preferred stock and then for common stock. Therefore, when an appraiser considers the value of those securities in turn, increasing attention must be given to the ability of the business to cover interest, preferred dividends, and common dividends because therein lies most of the risk associated with these different forms of investment. Therein also lies the essence of comparability in the market approach.

The value is calculated by capitalizing the preferred dividend at the yield rate of comparable preferred issues. The calculation is easy; the analysis of comparable issues is much more difficult than for debt securities.

Common Stock.   The valuation of common stock has been the subject of much study and there are excellent references available. It is a subject deserving of a complete book, and no attempt is made here to provide even the essence of it except to note the "high points" and to discuss those aspects that often lead to misunderstanding between appraiser and client.

Nearly always the appraiser is called upon to value closely held shares (not traded on a public market). These shares are similar to a parcel of land that has never been sold. The appraiser's approach is the same as for land—find comparable land that has sold recently and use that information. Unfortunately, establishing the comparability of land is usually easier than for shares of common stock. There are simply more variables involved.

The appraiser first analyzes the subject company to establish its primary characteristics, such as:

Industry classification	Capital structure
Product line(s)	Inventory turnover
Size	Liquidity
Sales growth	Interest coverage
Earnings growth	Amount of working capital
Variability in sales/earnings	Non-operating assets
Depreciation rates	
Effective tax rate	

These are just a few of the factors to be considered. Their use is intended to quantify the relative amounts of business and financial risk for the subject company.

The appraiser then reviews all available data on companies with similar characteristics whose common stock is publicly traded. This usually involves several iterations, each further winnowing the list of comparable companies. Techniques developed in financial analysis are used to facilitate the comparison and to quantify differences.

The data from these companies are used to develop market multiples that can in turn be used to value the subject common stock. These market multiples or ratios express the relationship between balance sheet and income statement items and the market price of common stock. They are applied to the corresponding items of the subject company to derive an indication of what the market price of its stock would be. These relationships typically include:

1. Price/earnings ratio (P/E).
2. Price/EBIT ratio.
3. Price/EBDIT ratio.
4. Price/cash flow.
5. Price/sales.
6. Price/common equity (also referred to as the market/book ratio [M/B].

Before the market multiples can be applied, the appraiser must go through an analysis and normalization process relative to the reported income of the subject company. This is the same task that was described above in the income approach section.

The result of a valuation by this methodology is an indication of value of a *minority* position in the subject company's common stock. A minority basis value is the result because the market multiples used are the result of exchanges of minority interests. The appraiser often must make adjustments in this value indication to reflect special conditions that exist with the subject stock. Some of these adjustments are presented in the sections that follow.

This is a difficult and demanding analysis and the reader should not infer otherwise from the shortness of this description.

Special Considerations

This section discusses certain aspects of both business enterprise and securities valuation that are often not well understood by those unfamiliar with valuation.

Degrees of Difficulty.   The development of a group of comparable companies is complex and requires a large amount of work. The amount of "conglomeration" in American industry adds to the difficulty, since it is increasingly difficult to locate comparables that are in a single line of business, as most appraisal subjects are. There is a wealth of information available about W. R. Grace, Textron, and ITT, but where can an appraiser use it?

It is more difficult to value the stock of a company that has multiple, and dissimilar, product lines or several divisions and/or subsidiaries. These may have to be treated as separate entities, and the effort becomes nearly the same as a separate appraisal of several independent entities. There may also be the added complexity of determining the actual earnings of business segments that are vertically integrated and between which there is a system of transfer prices.

A separate and additional valuation may be required when the subject business has an equity interest in another entity. If this is material, that interest should be valued and not merely reflected at its carrying cost.

Premium for Control.   There are several very judgmental issues concerning the valuation of common stock. This particular factor arises when the purpose of the valuation relates to the price that should be offered (by the buyer) or received (by the seller) for all, or a majority, of the common stock of a company. There are a number of reasons why such a buyer would offer a price higher than when small blocks of shares are traded:

1.   A buyer has to overcome the "inertia" of stockholders who are satisfied with their investment, as evidenced by the fact that they have not availed themselves of the ready market to sell.

2.   A buyer desires to acquire at least 80 percent of the outstanding shares so that financial results can be consolidated with those of the acquiring corporation for federal income tax purposes.

3.   A buyer does not want to be saddled with a lingering minority who might be disruptive in the future.

4.   A buyer recognizes the possibility for improved operations and earnings in the acquired business if total control is gained.

5.   A buyer desires to make an attractive offer that will reduce or eliminate competition, so as to avoid a bidding war that could further escalate the price.

There is no question that premiums are offered, and there are publications that track them. The question for the appraiser is, "How much should the premium be?" Most appraisers rely on the evidence of premiums that have been paid in the recent past, classifying the data by industry group or type of company to best match the evidence with the subject company.

A premium for control may also be considered in the valuation of a majority stockholding, even when the appraisal purpose is not for a buyout. Most would agree that there advantages to being the majority stockholder in a company, whether it is publicly traded or closely held. A majority shareholder can control the allocation of company resources and strategies, can cause the company assets to be liquidated, can control the sale of the enterprise, and can control the dividend policy. Control of a closely held company, therefore, affords the majority shareholder elements of liquidity that other shareholders do not have. If his investment is not going well, only the majority shareholder in such a company has the chance to "opt out" and invest the proceeds elsewhere.

There seems to be no additional value to be ascribed to the control of a publicly traded corporation, unless that majority is sufficient to unilaterally sell the company and obtain the premium from the buyer. This level of control probably requires an 80 percent holding. Without that shareholding, a majority stockholder in a public company has no more liquidity than any other stockholder. In addition, the courts have recognized the fiduciary responsibility of a majority shareholder to minority shareholders, and the opportunity to divert company resources to oneself is negligible.

Lack of Marketability/Liquidity. Obviously, this is the other side of the premium for control "coin." Minority shareholders in public companies do not suffer from liquidity problems unless, of course, their company goes into bankruptcy, is suspended from trading, and so on, in which case all shareholders have the same problem.

Minority shareholders in a closely held corporation, on the other hand, may have monumental liquidity problems because potential investors recognize the disadvantages of such a shareholding:

1. Inability to cause the company to be sold.
2. Inability to cause company assets to be liquidated.
3. May not receive financial statements of company performance.
4. No influence over dividend policy.

5. No knowledge of company resources that might be being diverted to the majority shareholder.

6. No recourse if company is mismanaged.

In short, the minority stockholder in a closely held corporation is "along for the ride" and cannot get off, no matter where it goes. Sometimes the only recourse is to become a "gadfly" to the extent that the majority buys out the interest.

The appraiser recognizes these factors by applying a discount to the equivalent value of a minority interest in a public corporation, where these problems do not exist. Such a discount can be as high as 70–80 percent.

Just as Revenue Ruling 59-60 set forth the criteria to be considered in the valuation of closely held stock, Revenue Ruling 77-287 followed with an excellent description of the investor problems associated with restricted securities, and the effect that those restrictions have on value. It is unusual that appraisers, financial analysts, and the IRS agree so well about a valuation matter:

> A variety of methods have been used by the securities industry to value restricted securities. The SEC (Securities and Exchange Commission) rejects all automatic or mechanical solutions to the valuation of restricted securities, and prefers, in the case of the valuation of investment company portfolio stocks, to rely upon good faith valuations by the board of directors of each company. The study made by the SEC found that restricted securities generally are issued at a discount from the market value of freely tradable securities.[4.03 Summary]

Appraisers also consider the size of a shareholding in the context of liquidity problems. Referred to as "blockage," this concept recognizes that the price obtained in the sale of a large block of a company's stock may be less than that which could be realized in smaller sales, because selling pressure on the market depresses the price. The owner of a block of stock might sell in small amounts over time to minimize the price drop. In either case, the present worth of the proceeds of sale is proportionately less than for a smaller shareholding sold as a block and therefore a discount is warranted.

An appraiser will also consider a discount on stock for which there are trading restrictions. These restrictions take many forms, but their essence is to preclude the owner from selling the shares for some period of time or to permit sale only under specific, controlled conditions. This is specifically addressed above.

Non-Operating Property. An appraiser will look for nonoperating or other property that is "excess" to the operating business. This can be any form of property: capital, tangible, or intangible. Most often, this is in the form of excess (by comparison with other, similar businesses) working capital or real estate.

The appraiser will segregate the value of this property *and* the income that it may produce from the operating business before valuing that business. The reason is that market multiples are intended to capitalize income produced by assets dedicated to a specific business. Stated another way, non-operating assets could be sold, and the proceeds distributed to stockholders, without impairing the earning capacity of the basic business.

Special Business Segments. Certain types of businesses present special challenges to the appraiser. These situations may require additional appraisal work effort and different demands for information from the client.

Holding Companies. A holding company's purpose is to own other operating businesses and/or property so as to "package" their ownership for its stockholders. A common type of holding company is one organized to own commercial real estate, though there are holding companies that represent the ownership of industrial corporations, agricultural real estate, shopping centers, and oil and gas development rights.

The sum of assets approach is the only practical way to value such an enterprise. This will require several individual appraisals, and may, in the examples above, require appraisal specialists.

It is very important to note that when appraising the *securities* of a holding company substantial discounts from the underlying asset value may still be in order because of the inability of a minority shareholder to effectuate a liquidation or because of the long liquidation period necessary for even the majority shareholder to realize the underlying asset value.

High-Tech Businesses. This type of enterprise is typically very dependent on patients, know-how, proprietary technology, research and development completed and underway, and an assembled workforce. In the valuation of such a company's stock, the appraiser must investigate these assets to a greater degree than normal in order to form an opinion as to their strengths and weaknesses and thereby evaluate the overall business risk of the enterprise.

Regulated Businesses.   Many businesses are subject to regulations that can affect their value. The classic case is a public utility, in which many aspects of business activity, including the price of products and services, are subject to regulation at the local, state, and/or federal level. Many common carriers are regulated as to form of services, routes, and territories, as are certain types of communications business.

These regulated industries present unique requirements for the appraiser to determine how, and to what extent, regulation affects the value of their securities (and assets, for that matter). Appraisals of regulated business require special knowledge on the part of the appraiser as to the specifics of regulation, current philosophy of the subject's regulatory body, recent decisions, and anticipated changes in the regulatory environment.

6

APPRAISING TANGIBLE ASSETS

Chapter 4 discussed the three basic valuation methods which are applicable to all types of property. This chapter covers methods most applicable to various kinds of tangible assets ("fixed assets") and some of the techniques used by the fixed asset appraiser.

TANGIBLE ASSETS DEFINED

When the terms "tangible asset" or "fixed asset" are used, they are intended to include property such as:

1. Land.
2. Land improvements.
3. Improvements to leased property.
4. Buildings.
5. Machinery and equipment.
6. Tooling, patterns, fixtures, molds.
7. Office furniture and equipment.
8. Vehicles.
9. Construction in progress.

Typically, this is property that is capitalized as "plant property and equipment" on the books of a business.

MARKET AND INCOME APPROACHES

Land, computer equipment, and vehicles are always appraised using the market and/or income approach. Special-purpose vehicles that have features not found in the market might be appraised using a combination of the market and cost approaches, but this is not common.

Real Estate

The valuation of real estate, as one component of the tangible assets of a business enterprise, is often based upon a mixture of techniques. As noted above, land is always valued by comparable sales. Land improvement and building classifications may be valued by the market, income, or cost approach, or all three.

When the property appraised is of a general-purpose type, such an office building, warehouse, or light manufacturing building with typical land improvements (parking lot, lighting, fencing, landscaping), the appraiser should utilize all three approaches to value the real-estate package.

When portions of the real-estate package are not in keeping with other properties in the market, these elements are appraised by the cost approach and their value is added to the market value of the "typical" package. Examples would include:

1. Unusual landscaping.
2. Excess railroad sidings, access roads, or utility services.
3. Special elevators, cranes, wiring, piping, cold rooms or laboratories within the building.

Whether these extra amenities add to the value of the real estate depends, in part, on the premise of value. If the premise is cost of reproduction or replacement, they should be included at their full share of value; likewise, if the premise is fair market value for continued use, these added features are in use and thus have value to the occupant of the property. If, on the other hand, the premise is fair market value for alternate use, these features may or may not add value to the property. This is analogous to constructing a pistol range in one's basement. It is unlikely that the market value of the home is increased by an amount equal to the cost of construction. Full value would only be realized if a prospective buyer is also a shooting enthusiast.

Other Assets

For other classifications of fixed assets, cost approach is the preferred method, with the market approach often used as a confirming technique. The following sections discuss three cost-approach techniques in common use: the trended original cost, inventory and unit cost, and unit of capacity techniques.

COST APPROACH

The following discussion addresses the determination of fair market value by the cost approach, since this is the most complex process. Other premises of value appear as components of this technique. Recall that the structure of this technique is as follows:

Cost of Reproduction New (CRN)

or

Cost of Replacement (COR)

Less:	Physical Depreciation
Less:	Functional Obsolescence
Equals:	Replacement Cost Less Depreciation (CORLD)
Less:	Economic Obsolescence
Equals:	FAIR MARKET VALUE

The cost-approach techniques described below have as their purpose the determination of one or another of the intermediate points in this calculation, typically either cost of reproduction or cost of replacement.

Trended Original Cost Technique

Sometimes referred to as "trending" or "indexing," this is a method of restating the cost of property from one time period to another. The appraiser uses trending to obtain the current (as of the appraisal date) cost of property by restating its original (purchase date) cost.

Reported changes in the "cost of living" result from the use of trending to quantify the changes in price of goods and services that affect our domestic life. This concept is not new; in 1780, Massachusetts soldiers were paid in notes, the value of which was to vary with the price of a selected group of commodities:

Both Principle and Interest to be paid in the then current Money of said State, in a greater or less Sum, according as Five Bushels of Corn, Sixty-eight Pounds and four-seventh Part of a Pound of Beef, Ten Pounds of SHEEP'S LEATHER shall then cost more or less, than One Hundred and Thirty Pounds current Money, at the then current Prices of said Articles.[1]

Properly applied, the trending of original cost can produce an accurate indication of current costs in a very economical fashion. What is required are appropriate trend factors and accurate costs by vintage year. This is one of the underlying considerations of FASB 33, discussed in Chapter 3.

Trend Factors.   Trend factors, or cost indexes, are constructed either by combining the price change of a group of commodities or by tracking the price change of a manufactured product.

For example, there are a number of published trends for building construction. These trends are themselves constructed by combining the price movements of the many labor and material elements that go into the construction of a building of a particular type. Such a trend might represent the combination of 50–100 individual price trends, weighted in the proportion that the cost of the individual components bear on the completed building. The weighting of these elements (brick, concrete, many labor crafts, steel, and so on) vary according to the building type.

For a manufactured product, it is most common to develop a price trend by following the price changes of a small number of typical units that do not change materially from year to year. Changes in product introduce complexities into the process of developing trends, but do not prevent it. One products that has remained nearly the same from Colonial times to the present is whiskey, and so a long and consistent price index is available.

A price index can be thought of as a series of percentages, expressed relative to a base year, and is calculated as shown in Table 6.1.

The term "price index" is used to denote an index series for an individual commodity or labor craft. Most often, appraisers use cost indexes, or trends, that are a combination of price indexes appropriate for the subject property. The appraiser's calculation begins with deriving a *translator* from the cost index. A translator is simply a factor that can be calculated from an index with *any base year* and that can be applied directly to calculate current cost in the desired year. This is shown in Table 6.2.

This brief explanation of the mechanics of developing a cost index serves to illustrate several important facts about trending:

TABLE 6.1

Year	Commodity Price (per pound) ($)	Price Index (1985 = 100)
1977	17.45	52.0
1978	19.62	58.4
1979	22.00	65.5
1980	23.15	68.9
1981	25.75	76.7
1982	24.58	73.2
1983	26.70	79.5
1984	29.45	87.7
1985	33.58	100.0
1986	35.90	106.9
1987	36.00	107.2

1. A cost index must be specific to its purpose. A cost index of the composite costs for a masonry building is inappropriate to use for a steel structure. The Consumer Price Index is too general to use for a sewing machine.

2. Cost indexes can be geographical in scope. This was especially true in years past, when labor rates and material prices varied considerably across the country.

TABLE 6.2

Year	Cost Index (1985 = 100)	Translator (1987 = 1.000)
1977	49.2	2.201
1978	51.3	2.111
1979	60.0	1.805
1980	65.4	1.656
1981	68.7	1.576
1982	73.4	1.475
1983	76.2	1.421
1984	84.1	1.288
1985	100.0	1.083
1986	103.2	1.049
1987	108.3	1.000

TABLE 6.3

Year	Original Cost ($)	Translator	1987 Cost Level ($)
1977	12,485	2.201	27,479
1978	3,421	2.111	7,222
1979	819	1.805	1,478
1980	6,232	1.656	10,320
1981	42,800	1.576	67,453
1982	15,850	1.475	23,379
1983	102,003	1.421	144,946
1984	8,421	1.288	10,846
1985	10,500	1.083	11,372
1986	11,657	1.049	12,228
1987	3,343	1.000	3,343

3. Cost indexes are useful only when they apply to the time period needed. It is very risky to extrapolate back or forward from known data or to fill in gaps by interpolating, because price movements do not always follow predictable patterns.

Calculating Value. The application of these translators to a series of original costs will restate the costs to the base year of the translator, for example, 1987, as illustrated on Table 6.3.

The 1987 cost level in Table 6.3 is the "Cost of Reproduction New" of the property represented by the costs in the years acquired. It is possible that the result of this process is replacement cost if the cost index follows the price of whatever commodity is capable of producing a given level of service (recalling the definitions of CRN and COR in Chapter 4). This is unusual, however, and the usual assumption is that the product of this calculation is CRN.

A cost index is also used by an appraiser to restate costs to a *prior* level. This technique is often used in the reconstruction of property records when an original cost in a previous year must be estimated. This calculation is illustrated in Table 6.4.

Original Costs. The validity of the value indication in Table 6.3 is dependent upon the extent to which the original cost amounts are representative of actual costs in the respective year. If the costs represent the purchase of

TABLE 6.4   Backtrended Cost

	Cost Index
1984	123.1
1983	115.0
1982	112.9
1981	106.8
1980	100.0
1979	98.6
1978	95.0
1977	95.0
1976	90.9
1975	86.7

1984 Cost = \$292.46

1978 Cost = \$225.69

$$\text{Translator} = \frac{1978 \text{ Cost Index}}{1984 \text{ Cost Index}}$$

$$= \frac{95.0}{123.0}$$

$$= 0.7717$$

$$\text{Backtrended Cost} \quad \underset{\$292.46}{\underline{1984}} \times \underset{0.7717}{} = \underset{\$225.69}{\underline{1978}}$$

worn-out equipment that was later rebuilt, used equipment, a bargain purchase, or an allocation of acquisition costs, the calculated value will be inaccurate.

The costs also must be specific as to the type of property they represent. If they are for an aggregation of buildings, machinery, and whatever, a trend series will not be representative.

It is also very critical that the vintage years be accurate. If retirements of property have not been reflected in the proper year, there may be "old dollars" in the original costs that should not be there. Given the typical movement of prices over the years, "old dollars" produce high current values. Another common situation is for a company to make an inventory in order to "clean up" its property record and to date all of the property in existence at that time with a common year of acquisition. The vintage year in the record is therefore not the year of purchase but the year the *record* was started. Obviously this is not a suitable basis for trending.

Before utilizing the trending technique, an appraiser will analyze the property record to determine whether it is a reasonably accurate basis on which to perform these calculations. It may be necessary to make spot checks in the plant to determine this.

Summary.   Advantages of the trended original-cost technique include:

1. It is a low-cost method of obtaining the value of fixed assets. When the client has a computerized fixed-asset record, this technique is greatly facilitated, and the line-by-line application of cost indexes and depreciation factors moves very quickly.
2. The calculation of gains and/or losses and tax recapture liability is greatly facilitated because there is a value calculated for each and every item in the property record.
3. When an accurate property record is available as a base and is applied appropriately, it produces an accurate result. Utility property is often valued by this technique because regulatory requirements assure an accurate property record and because tracking of costs by the industry makes good price trends available.
4. It is an accepted technique and there are many sources of price trend data, including publications of the U.S. government.

Disadvantages of the trended original-cost technique include:

1. Values of individual property units may not be as precise as with other methods.
2. It is depenent on the accuracy of the property record.
3. It cannot be universally applied.
4. Property more than 50 years old is difficult to trend accurately. This limitation may not apply to building structures, bridges, or dams for which there has been little change in construction methodology.

The reader should be aware of a number of points relative to the use of the trended original-cost technique:

1. It is essential to assess the form and content of the property record as to suitability as a basis for the procedure and accuracy of the result.

   Previously expensed property is not on the books and will therefore not be appraised. Policies relative to expenditures as capital or as expense may have changed through the years so that the property record at any given point is not consistent about what property is included and what is excluded.

   Some companies have a policy of *retiring* assets that become *fully depreciated* (the entire capital cost has been recovered on the accounting records) even though they may still be in use. Such assets would not be included in a trended original-cost appraisal, since it is based upon the property record.

   Property not recorded at actual cost will not be valued accurately. This would include property purchased used, not at-arm's length, or whose cost is the result of a previous allocation of purchase price.

   An *acquisition date* that does not reflect the asset's true age will result in inaccurate value. A typical example would be the previous purchase of an entire plant in which all assets were recorded with a common date of acquisition, regardless of their actual vintage year.

   A *record that combines* several types of property in a single line item is not suitable for trending because a single trend factor may not be available to reflect such an aggregation of property types. An example is a property record entry such as "Expansion project for #5 bottling line" (which might include building construction, wiring, piping, and machinery.

2. Land, other kinds of real estate, and vehicles should not be trended, even if there are price trends available that purport to apply. Their value is too dependent on outside variables that have nothing to do with price movements.

3. Equipment that is subject to a high degree of technological obsolescence can be trended, but caution is advised because values can move quickly and in unexpected directions. Computer equipment is a good example.

Inventory and Unit Cost Technique

This technique begins with a complete inventory of all property to be included in the appraisal. Each property item in this inventory is then priced at a current level and individually analyzed as to physical and functional depreciation.

Inventory. An effective inventory requires advance planning and careful execution by personnel who are trained in inventory procedures, who can properly identify the property units, and who know the subsequent appraisal steps. Clients sometimes express an interest in taking on this task as a "do-it-yourself" project to reduce appraisal costs. With rare exceptions, this should be discouraged.

An inventory is labor intensive and, because of that, must be done right the first time. Descriptions must be consistent and nomenclature correct, and essential information must be recorded to price the inventory accurately in a later step. An experienced appraiser once told of a trainee who, assigned to inventory the piping in a large power plant, came back with a one-line entry, "1 lot of pipe—damn big stuff."

Even with property as common as office furniture, an accurate description is essential. A "black file cabinet" cannot be priced without knowing whether it is wood or metal, locking, fireproof, letter or legal size, lateral, two- or four-drawer, and so on. Inventory work has the appearance of simplicity, but it is difficult to accomplish the task so that the product is useful in the appraisal process.

Property Units. The level of detail must be defined because this determines what the ultimate record will contain and greatly affects the effort required for the inventory.

A typical inventory work plan would specify that all machinery and equipment over some dollar value *or* cost (say, $5,000) would be recorded individually, whereas property classifications under the limit would be grouped. An individual machine unit might be described as:

Milling Machine, Kearney & Trecker, plain, horizontal, Model 25HP-SCK, s/n 1638574-11, knee type with support, motor drive coolant pump, motor drives and control.

A group category would be recorded as:

Plant furniture and equipment including desks, tables, chairs, drafting tables, storage cabinets, filing cabinets, calculators, copying and postage machines.

Setting this limit should be a thoughtful process, and guidance should be sought from the appraisal professional or sales representative. An appraisal inventory is the same as setting up a computerized database. It is costly to do in the first instance, and reformatting it in the future can range from exceedingly costly to prohibitive. It pays to think ahead about:

1. The ease of future property record-keeping.
2. Possible disposal of units, production lines, plants, divisions.
3. The cost of maintaining the system (the more detail, the more cost).
4. Capital recovery policies and differences in the economic life of various assets.
5. Cost accounting requirements.

Property Classifications. The discussion thus far has been in terms of broad property groupings, such as land improvements. Many businesses add further subdivisions, such as landscaping, roads, parking lots, railroad sidings, or yard lighting.

Within a classification such as "Machinery and Equipment," there may be additional groupings of power wiring, process piping (i.e., air, chilled water, gases), Plant Equipment (i.e., racks, pallets, scales, small tools, and so on).

Within a classification such as "Tooling," which might also include patterns, fixtures, molds, or drawings, there may be a real benefit to segregation by *product line* because of differences in economic life and the future ability to retire assets on a specific basis. If, at the time of an appraisal you already have a chart of accounts that defines property classifications, this should be communicated to the appraiser before the inventory begins. This would also be true if you are acquiring a business that uses a different set of classifications.

If you do not have detailed classifications or would like to change your system, now is the time to plan it with the appraiser. Refer back to the criteria discussed under the definition of property units for some reasons why additional classifications of property can be helpful. Other reasons include the need to segregate insurable and non-insurable assets and assets not subject to local property taxes.

Access. The appraiser will need complete access to all property locations. Where these locations are unattended, the appraiser will need to be accompanied or provided with a key and an authorizing document.

The appraisal team may be on-site for several days and may require a place to work where drawings and other records can be spread out and to keep their work materials. It is helpful if access can be provided after regular working hours because some equipment inspections are best carried out when the unit is not in operation.

Plant Personnel.   The appraisal team will need access to engineering and/or operating personnel in order to determine equipment ages, maintenance histories, operating efficiencies, extent of custom designs and modifications, and so on.

Plant Records.   Purchase documents and the property record should be available, along with invoices, budgets, project plans (especially for custom-designed or process machinery and equipment).

Property Ownership.   The appraiser should be informed about the ownership of property that may be on your premises. Remember that some leased property must be insured and therefore should be included in an appraisal for that purpose. The appraiser will also need to know about owned property that is *not* on your premises, such as tooling or molds that are with vendors. Access will be necessary at those locations as well as your own.

Pricing the Inventory.   The appraiser will price the completed inventory using one or two of several sources available: catalogs and price lists from manufacturers and dealers and, for large or special-purpose machinery, price quotes directly from their source. Machinery and equipment appraisers also keep abreast of activity in the used-equipment market and at auctions, often attending sales and auctions in order to observe personally the market activity and asking and selling prices.

The total value of a property unit may comprise several elements, such as:

1.   The base machine unit from the manufacturer or dealer, or the individual components such as motors, pumps, piping, structural steel, concrete, and so on.

2.   Freight charges to bring the unit to the appraised site.

3.   Installation labor, which might involve a number of crafts.

4.   Design and construction of accessory equipment when an individual machine unit becomes part of an integrated manufacturing process.

5.   Design engineering, purchasing, plant layout, safety engineering, materials handling, and environmental compliance costs.

6.   Costs associated with testing and run-in of machine units and process equipment before manufacturing standards are met.

An appraiser will typically express these additional "soft" costs as a percentage of the base machine unit cost. These costs will vary substantially from industry to industry and can, in some instances, equal the base machinery cost.

Summary.   Advantages of the inventory/unit cost approach include:

1. It assures the user that all property will be included, whether it was previously recorded on the company's books or not. It also ensures that unrecorded retirements will be excluded.
2. It provides a more detailed basis for applying depreciation.
3. It provides more precise values on individual property units.
4. It provides the means to structure a meaningful property record.
5. It provides more detailed information on individual property units.

Disadvantages of this technique include:

1. It is the most costly and time-consuming technique.
2. It requires more skill on the part of the appraiser and the availability of extensive pricing data.
3. There is the potential for disruptions in plant routine because of the inspection requirements.

Unit of Capacity Technique

The cost approach by this technique determines replacement cost directly and is useful in industries where the manufacture of certain basic materials or commodities is such that it requires a standard complement of property. Therefore the current cost per unit of output can be estimated within a reasonably narrow range. Examples would be: water or wastewater treatment; electric-power generation; basic process industries such as steel, aluminum, petro-chemical manufacture, refining, and concrete.

The product of this technique is replacement cost, because these measures come from currently completed construction projects and no one is building obsolete plants, presumably. Unit of capacity measures are meaningful because, in the industries where they are used, by far the largest investment for productive capacity is in the machinery and equipment or specialized structures. Investment in land or intangible assets, for example, would be quite low by comparison and these types of asset can vary considerably in value. Therefore the cost of a plant of given capacity will be consistent and unit of capacity measures will have utility.

This cost-approach technique is used by appraisers as a primary measure only when the appraisal purpose is to determine a broad range of value. Most often it is used as a confirming technique for value indications determined by other means.

Unit of capacity measures should be distinguished from so-called rules of thumb, and there are many of those. There are rules of thumb for such diverse situations as the cost per seat to construct various types of restaurants or theaters, the value per patient in a dental practice, and the cost per pupil for an elementary-school building. These are rules of thumb and must be recognized and used as such.

Depreciation

By using these three cost-approach techniques, the appraiser obtains an indication of value *before* a consideration of depreciation. Depending on where the particular cost-approach technique left us in the formula, one or more elements of depreciation need to be reflected:

Cost of Reproduction New (CRN)

or

Cost of Replacement (COR)

Less:	Physical Depreciation
Less:	Functional Obsolescence
Equals:	Replacement Cost Less Depreciation (CORLD)
Less:	Economic Obsolescence
Equals:	FAIR MARKET VALUE

An accurate value conclusion is just as dependent on a proper estimate of appraisal depreciation as it is on a careful calculation of cost of replacement, and a significant part of the appraiser's work will be devoted to an analysis of all forms of depreciation evidenced by the subject property. This is especially true in a multi-location, multi-product-line business. The appraiser's analysis will include:

1. Inspections of the property to observe the extent of physical deterioration.
2. Development of estimates of repair costs for those depreciation elements that are judged to be *curable*.
3. Quantification of those depreciation elements that are judged to be *incurable* by, for example, calculating the present worth of excess operating costs where a replacement property is more economical to run.
4. Analyzing maintenance and repair expenses.
5. Reviewing records of production costs, speeds, and down time.
6. Observing current and intended future hours of operation, production quantities, capital budgets, and other plans for change in operations.
7. Observing unusual operating conditions (corrosive atmosphere, abrasive materials, and so on).
8. Investigating environmental conditions that may require correction.
9. Comparing operations and equipment to "state of the art" conditions within the industry.

This type of investigation will equip the appraiser to make estimates of physical and functional depreciation relative to the various classifications of property. The resulting analysis will be utilized by the appraiser in various ways, depending on the cost-approach technique utilized.

When the trending technique is used, all three forms of depreciation must be applied, with the possible exception of functional obsolescence when replacement cost is established directly. It is common to combine a factor to reflect physical depreciation with the price trend factor, since this can logically be tied to chronological age. For example, assume that a five-year-old asset is to be trended and depreciated in a single calculation. If ten years is the normal life for this asset and physical depreciation is determined to occur in a straight-line pattern, then physical depreciation is 50 percent (5/10 years) and the value calculation would be as follows:

$$\frac{\text{Original Cost}}{\$1,200.00} \times \frac{\text{Translator}}{1.685} \times \frac{\text{Depreciation Factor}}{0.50} = \frac{\text{Value}}{\$1,011.00}$$

In using the trending technique, the appraiser will often develop several series of depreciation factors. Since most trended original-cost valuations are done by computer, these tables of depreciation factors may be stored and used by the computer according to an asset's age and account classification.

Functional obsolescence may not be appropriate to apply according to age and would be more likely applied to property groups or locations. Even when using the trended original-cost technique, an appraiser will often inspect selected locations or types of property in order to increase the precision of the depreciation estimate. For individual locations or types of property that do not fit the depreciation tables, the appraiser will make special adjustments in the computer-generated values to reflect this situation.

Physical and functional depreciation is reflected in an inventory and unit cost assignment from information gathered in the inventory phase relative to property on a unit-by-unit basis. These factors are not always applied on an individual unit basis, but the information is accumulated that way.

Economic obsolescence always comes from an evaluation of outside factors and the economic viability of the business. The myriad of factors affecting this element of depreciation are discussed in Chapter 5. When the premise of value is fair market value on a continued use basis, the appraiser of the tangible assets must consider this element of depreciation. He or she can recognize it by analyzing outside economic factors and the financial performance of the subject business (or utilize this information from another member of the appraisal team), *or* state in the report that the financial viability of the business was *assumed* and that no such studies were made.

To perform an appraisal for this purpose and be silent on this element of depreciation would be unethical because it could lead to a serious misunderstanding about what the conclusion of value represents.

Market Confirmation

As noted above, when the appraiser is utilizing one of these techniques in a cost approach, there will almost always be some use of a market approach, either to supplement cost data or to confirm cost-based conclusions. One must keep in mind that the cost approach is used as a surrogate for the market in those cases for which an appropriate market does not exist. Thus appraisers often attend sales and auctions of machinery in order to gather data that they can use to test their conclusions of "cost less all forms of depreciation." The purpose of their analysis is to test the techniques used for "no market" property with data from cases where there is a market.

A note of caution should be injected as to the interpretation of data from the used-equipment market. These principles are well known to appraisers but less so to those outside the profession:

1. When one observes a price *to a dealer* or the price a dealer would offer to purchase some equipment installed at a plant site ("as is, where is") that amount is analogous to *orderly liquidation value*.

   This amount is for the base machine *without* freight, installation, engineering, and so on (since the dealer is not going to compensate the former owner for these costs) and *less* the dealer's cost to dismantle, remove, and transport the unit *plus* the dealer's overhead and profit. These costs may be considerable because the dealer's holding period may be long.

2. When "to a dealer" price data relate to a situation in which a dealer makes an offer for all the equipment in a plant as a package, it is most similar to *forced* liquidation or tantamount to an auction. This is based on the assumption that the dealer probably does not want all the equipment and is taking the bad with the good, knowing that some of it will be very difficult or impossible to sell.

3. When one observes price data "from a dealer" (the price one would have to pay to a dealer), this is analogous to the price that would be paid to a manufacturer if the manufacturer sold used equipment. It is theoretically the same amount one would conclude from starting with cost of reproduction new and properly quantifying physical and functional depreciation.

   This amount, together with all the costs of freight, installation, engineering, and so on is representative of *fair market value* in continued use (assuming adequate earnings).

Summary

The tangible asset appraiser has, within the three valuation methods, several techniques for reaching a competent conclusion. Sometimes the method and technique are dictated by the type of property and at times they are dictated by the purpose of the appraisal. There is nearly always some latitude, however, and the client should participate in decision making about the choice of technique. This will greatly enhance the client's understanding of the valuation product.

There can be a "mix and match" of techniques to fit the circumstances, such as:

1. Inventory the large location(s) and use trending for small, outlying sites.

2. Inventory the large dollar property classifications and trend those with smaller unit value.

3. Trend all property, then evaluate the results and do inventory work as required in special-purpose, old, or otherwise unusual locations.

4. Trend all property, since most of the value may be in intangible assets.

The client's concern should be to receive the maximum amount of valuation consulting relative to cost, given the requirements of the work. The client and appraiser should work together to design an appraisal service that will "put the effort (and fee) where the value is"—or where value issues may arise in the future. A competent appraiser knows these different techniques and can explain their advantages, disadvantages, strengths, and weaknesses. He or she also knows how they can be properly applied within professional and ethical standards. Together you can develop the appropriate combination for your particular situation.

REFERENCE

1. Quoted from John I. Griffin, *Statistics*. New York: Holt, Rinehart & Winston, 1962.

7

THE VALUATION OF INTANGIBLE ASSETS

Every business enterprise has a complement of intangible assets. As noted in an earlier chapter, appraisers of 25 years ago lumped the intangible assets together as "goodwill." There has been a continuing effort in the intervening years to analyze that lump and to develop methods to individually value its components.

In some companies, intangible assets are the main driving force, whereas in others they are of relatively little importance. Intangible assets typically do not appear on a company's balance sheet unless they were acquired individually or as part of a business combination. One occasionally observes intangible assets such as patents, copyrights, or computer software on a balance sheet. The amount recorded is nearly always the *cost* of development, not the value of the asset.

Intangible assets are valued using the three basic methods described in Chapter 4. There are, as with tangible assets, certain specialized techniques that the appraiser uses within this theoretical framework.

Intangible Assets Defined

There is no absolutely clear definition of what constitutes an intangible asset within a business enterprise. A dictionary might define intangible property as "having no physical substance" or as being "not detectable to the senses." Accounting theory discusses intangibles as assets that do not have physical substance, that grant rights and privileges to a business owner, that are in-

129

separable from the enterprise, or as assets for which the determination and timing of future benefits is very difficult. Every definition seems to have one or another shortcoming.

For the purpose of this book, intangible assets are defined as all elements of a business enterprise that remain after tangible assets are removed. They are the elements, after working capital and fixed assets, that "make the business go" and contribute to its earning power. Their existence is tied to the presence, or expectation, of earnings and, recalling Figure 5.3, they appear last in the development of a business and disappear first in its demise.

The Financial Accounting Standards Board has written:

> Future economic benefit is the essence of an asset. . . . Uncertainty about business and economic outcomes often clouds whether or not particular items that might be assets have the capacity to provide future economic benefits to the entity. . . , sometimes precluding their recognition as assets. . . . For example, business enterprises engage in research and development activities, advertise, develop markets, open new branches or divisions, and the like, and spend significant funds to do so. The uncertainty is not about the intent to increase future economic benefits but about whether and, if so, to what extent they succeeded in doing so.[1]

This thinking guides an accountant who must decide whether an expenditure should be expensed or capitalized, and this decision must be made at the time the expenditure is made, obviously when uncertainty is greatest. The appraiser has the benefit of hindsight and can judge whether these expenditures did in fact create assets capable of producing future economic benefits to the enterprise. This is the essence of appraising the intangible assets of a business.

Reasons for Intangible Asset Valuation

Intangible assets may be valued in connection with:

1. An exchange in which intangibles are transferred between companies.
2. In an allocation of purchase price, when all the assets of a business, both tangible and intangible, are valued.
3. In support of the determination of royalty rates or license fees.
4. To substantiate a loss due to abandonment or casualty.

5. In support of a business enterprise valuation.

6. Their use as collateral in financing.

Exchange. In an exchange or when intangible assets are contributed as part of a joint venture, the buyer or seller may want to have an independent opinion of value.

Allocation of Purchase Price. Most knowledge developed by appraisal practitioners on the subject of intangible asset valuation is a result of appraisals for allocation of purchase price. In such an allocation it is the buyer's desire to maximize future tax deductions by identifying and valuing all assets that are subject to depreciation (or amortization, in the case of intangibles). Depreciation has been a part of taxation for many years, but Section 167 of the 1954 Internal Revenue Code clarified many issues, including the amortization of intangible assets. Section 1.167(a)–3 provides that:

> If an intangible asset is known from experience or other factors to be of use in the business or in the production of income for only a limited period, the length of which can be estimated with reasonable accuracy, such an intangible asset may be the subject of a depreciation allowance. Examples are patents and copyrights. An intangible asset, the useful life of which is not limited, is not subject to an allowance for depreciation. . . . No deduction for depreciation is allowable with respect to goodwill. . . .

With this economic incentive in place, appraisers began to examine and analyze what was previously treated as "goodwill" in order to discover those elements that could be identified, individually valued, and for which a finite remaining life could be "estimated with reasonable accuracy."

There are many issues relating to the valuation of intangibles and to the support necessary for amortization, and these subjects have been the focus of much litigation. For additional information on this complex subject, the reader is directed to the many tax reference books and periodicals available.

License Agreements. The valuation of intangible assets for the support of license fees is less known and a more recent development. Just as the amount of rent charged for building occupancy relates to the value of the real estate, the value of an intangible asset conveyed to a licensee ought to be commensurate with the license fee or royalty rate. When the rights to an intangible asset are transferred between taxing jurisdictions, such as between countries, the amount of royalties paid may become an issue with one or the other of the taxing authorities involved because the payment of royalties is usually a tax-deductible expense.

Abandonment or Loss.   Take the example of a large corporation that needs to value the goodwill of a number of businesses acquired in the 1920s. This corporation had entered on its balance sheet a large amount of goodwill for many acquisitions over the years, and it had become impossible to trace the source of the entries. A number of the acquired companies had been sold or no longer existed, and some portion of the goodwill needs to be valued so it can be written off.

Even if an intangible asset cannot be amortized, there may be a benefit to determining its value at the time of acquisition. It certainly is less costly and more accurate to do it then than 60 years later.

Intangible assets are subject to unforeseen loss and damage litigation; for example, litigation regarding the value of a company's database of customer information which was copied and obtained by a competitor. There are many cases of patent and trademark infringement in which the value of the underlying intangible asset is at issue.

Business Enterprise Support.   An appraiser will occasionally value the significant intangible assets of an enterprise as a confirming technique and to support a business enterprise value determined by other means. An example is in the case of a start-up enterprise of a type for which there are no comparable companies.

Collateral.   Frequently, intangible assets are being considered by lenders as collateral. This is happening more often because there are an increasing number of businesses whose primary earning power comes from their intangible assets and because lenders are becoming comfortable with the concept.

INTANGIBLE ASSET CLASSIFICATIONS

Intangible assets can be categorized and, in doing so, made more understandable, for example:

1.   Rights.
2.   Knowledge.

3.   Soft tangibles.
4.   Relationships.
5.   Unidentifiable.

Rights

Every business enterprise acquires rights by establishing agreements with other businesses, individuals, or governmental bodies. At the very minimum, a business establishes its right to carry on operations through licensing or registration at the local government level. A large enterprise may have a "bundle of rights" comprised of thousands of elements.

Contractual Rights.   These exist according to the terms of a written contract which defines the parties to the agreement, the nature of the rights transferred, the transfer consideration, and the duration of the agreement. A contract can be appraised either on behalf of the company *receiving* the goods or services or the one *providing* them.

Receiving Contracts.   The existence per se of a contract does not necessarily indicate the presence of a valuable intangible asset. Value arises because the contract contains favorable elements. A method to help identify favorable contracts negotiated in the past is to compare them to recently negotiated contracts of a similar nature. Valuation is nearly always by an income approach, because the favorable elements are quantified in terms of an income stream. Any contract for goods or services can have value, though the most common would include:

1.   Leases of premises at terms better than available in the current market. This is the most commonly valued contract and an advantageous lease is called a *leasehold interest,* because the lessee obtains an interest in the property during the period of the lease. These can be as ordinary as for office space or as exotic as for a satellite transponder.
2.   Distribution agreements for the sale, warehousing, and movement of products.
3.   Employment contracts that act to retain key personnel.
4.   Financing arrangements that result in funds being available at favorable terms or at lower rates than otherwise.
5.   Insurance coverage at better than market rates.

6. Contracts for the supply of raw materials or purchased products.
7. Contracts for services such as equipment maintenance, data processing, or utility services.
8. Licenses or governmental certifications where these are in short supply or, unavailable.
9. Rights to receive goods or services in limited supply, such as broadcast network affiliations or film distribution rights.
10. Covenants by a former owner or employee not to compete.

Providing Contracts.   These do not necessarily need to have advantageous elements to have value within an enterprise. As long as they have the capability of providing a positive earnings stream that exceeds what is required to provide a return on the other assets employed, they are likely to have value. This type of contract may include:

1. Mortgage servicing rights to collect, process, and manage escrow and insurance matters on a portfolio of mortgages.
2. Loan agreements in which there will be a return of principal and interest in the future.
3. Agreements to provide food service, health care, data processing, advertising, or other consulting services.
4. Agreements to provide goods under contract for future delivery.
5. Student enrollments or subscriptions that are prepaid.

Prior Development Rights.   These exist because the company obtained exclusive rights to some innovation under the law.

Patents.   When addressing the nature of the intangible assets of an enterprise, the first category that comes to mind is patents. A patent is a right, granted by the government, to exclude others from using, selling, or copying an invention. In the United States, that right is granted for a period of 17 years.

Many patents have little or no value. Very few patents really protect a product, a design, a manufacturing process, or a material to the extent that competition is completely blocked. There are some notable exceptions, of course. A strong patent protects products or processes that are current and preserves their market. If it has been the successful subject of infringement litigation, its value is enhanced.

Often patents protect only a portion of a process, so that it becomes possible to design "around" them. Some patent owners, especially in the electronics industry, know that their protection can be evaded and that near infringement will result. In such cases the patents are used as bargaining chips to negotiate cross-licenses.

Copyrights.   A copyright is similar to a patent and applies to the expression of an idea (rather than the idea itself) in written form, as artwork, as musical composition, as videotape or movie film, or as a computer program. In the United States, copyright protection is granted for a period equal to the life of the author plus 50 years or for either 75 or 100 years in the case of works written for hire.

The value of a copyright is based on the extent to which the owner is able to obtain income from the direct exploitation of the material or, through royalties, from the exploitation of the material by others.

When computer software is protected by copyright, it is usually in source-code form but, since a copyright protects only the "expression" of an idea and not the idea itself, many prefer to treat software as a trade secret. This is because copyrights (as patents) are public documents and, while the exact software source-code could not be reproduced, their examination might reveal programming techniques that would be useful to competitors.

Trademarks.   A trademark as defined in the Trademark Act of 1946 "includes any word, name, symbol, or device or any combination thereof adopted and used by a manufacturer or merchant to identify his goods and distinguish them from those manufactured by others." Rights are obtained by continued use and, when that use includes trade regulated by the federal government, the trademark may be registered by the Patent Office. Registration remains in force for 20 years and may be renewed for additional 20-year periods as long as the trademark is in use in commerce.

Technically, trademarks are used to identify goods and "service marks" identify services. They are identical except for this. In common usage both are referred to as "trademarks."

The most common trademarks are some form of company name, usually in distinctive type style, or a logo. Trademarks can also apply to distinctive shapes (of a package, for instance), a building style, or a color combination.

The function of a trademark is to authenticate the origin of goods or services so that the buyer can select those seen in advertisements or previously purchased. Thus they can be thought of as a "guarantee" of a certain level of quality or performance. A well-recognized trademark is, then, an asset that can be of considerable value to an enterprise.

A "trade name" is the name of a business, association, or other organization used to identify it. It cannot be registered at the federal level unless it is also a trademark. Ownership is governed by common or state law. A trade name is typically not an asset of material value since the buying public recognizes goods and services by their trademark and, in many cases, can be entirely unaware of the actual name of the producing company.

Knowledge

This category of intangible assets consists of facts and information assembled, organized and maintained by an enterprise in order to enhance its earning power. Typically, this is information that is protected from outsiders by confidential treatment.

Trade Secrets.   Often referred to as "know-how", "proprietary technology" or "secret processes," trade secrets have been defined (in Section 4 of the Uniform Trade Secret Act) as:

> . . . information, including a formula, pattern, compilation, program, device, method, technique or process that: (i) derives independent value, actual or potential, from not being generally known to, and not being readily ascertainable by proper means by, other persons who can obtain economic value from its disclosure or use, and (ii) is the subject of efforts that are reasonable under the circumstances to maintain its secrecy.

Some trade secrets are patentable inventions that have not been patented in order to protect the basic knowledge that a patent would reveal or to extend the economic life of the knowledge through secrecy. These are potentially the most valuable. Another trade secret is a compilation of information that *could* be assembled by another but has value to its owner because others have not compiled the data or because this would be too costly.

Embedded Know-How.   Know-how is often embodied in other assets and its existence can be overlooked.

Tangible Assets.   A highly specialized machine includes considerable know-how in the form of custom design or in the adjustments and modifications that were made over an extended run-in period. This activity often results from the difficulties encountered in taking a working process from the laboratory or pilot plant into production. Getting a machine to produce on the factory floor requires the knowledge and skills of many people. When manual operations are mechanized (such as the programming and testing of a robotic welder), know-how becomes a part of a tangible asset.

Computer Software. Computer programs very often contain the knowledge and experience of people. Software is classified as a "soft tangible" and further discussion is found below.

Compilations of Data. Collections of data are one form of trade secret, even if the data do not represent a patentable invention. In order to be of material value, compilations of data must be organized and accessible and (with the exception of historically significant information) should pertain to or be useful in current and future operations. Such data bases might include:

1. Research and development information such as laboratory logs, experiment designs, and results.
2. Results of product or material tests.
3. Results of market surveys or consumer testing.
4. Recipes for food products.
5. Formulas.
6. Job files, such as for consulting engagements or construction projects.

Secrecy. It is very important to remember that for a trade secret to have significant value it must be a *secret*. An appraiser will investigate the extent to which there are safeguards present to ensure that such information does not become public. These safeguards would include restricted access, requirements for confidentiality agreements, fragmenting the data so that only very few know it all, and the like.

Soft Tangible Assets

These consist of assets that have physical substance but are usually not classified as fixed assets. Often these are assets created by an investment that was accounted for as a current expense rather than being capitalized at the time it was made.

Computer Software. Revenue Procedure 69-21 (1969-2 CB 303) defines computer software to include:

> . . . all programs or routines used to cause a computer to perform a desired task or set of tasks, and the documentation required to describe and maintain those programs. Computer programs of all classes, for example, operating systems, executive systems, monitors, compilers and translators, assembly routines, and utility programs as well as application programs are included. "Computer software" does not include procedures which are external to the computer operations, such as instructions to transcription operators and external control procedures.

This can be a very significant intangible asset, and an appraiser will categorize it as being either *product* or *operational* software.

Product Software. A product of the subject company developed for resale to its customers, this can be individual, stand-alone programs or more complex modular systems that interface with one another. The software may be sold with or without consultant support and related services.

Operational Software. Used by the company in its own internal operations, operational software may have been purchased by the company, be used under license, developed by an outside firm under contract, or developed internally.

> *System Software.* (Sometimes called "the operating system") is required by the computer hardware to operate. Usually obtained from the hardware vendor as part of the computer system, it is rarely developed, though it may be modified, by the user.

> *Applications Software.* Used for the specific functions of the business. This might include:
> 1. Basic accounting functions such as general ledger, payroll, accounts payable and receivable, material and supplies and inventory control, and fixed-asset accounting. These systems are often purchased and may or may not have been extensively modified.
> 2. Company-specific accounting systems such as for sales and commissions, product costing, purchasing and customer billing. These would usually be developed in-house.

3. Management systems such as for personnel functions, property taxes, database systems for management information, property lease systems, word processing, or financial models.

4. Production systems such as for manufacturing scheduling, CAD-CAM, design models, engineering calculations, numerically controlled machines, and robotic operations.

Recalling the previous discussion of know-how, note that when (1) computer software is designed in-house and (2) it becomes more company specific in its design and function, it is likely to embody more know-how. That is, it is likely that more time was spent by "users" in the development, design, and testing of the system. When the users of the system are heavily involved in the design, more of their knowledge will be embodied in the system.

Computer software is classified as a "soft tangible" because it is intellectual property which is always in some physical form, such as a paper listing, magnetic tape, or floppy disk. Because of this dual nature, software has been the focus of much controversy relative to taxation as property by local and state governments. An appraisal for this purpose must begin with research into applicable case law in the subject jurisdiction to obtain the "ground rules" of the moment.

Specialized Databases. Many enterprises have developed specialized databases that contribute to present or future earnings, such as:

1. Advertising programs and materials that might include theme development, media commitments, printed matter, and videotapes.
2. A newspaper "morgue" of past issues.
3. A technical library of specialized materials.
4. Engineering specifications and drawings.
5. Service and training materials.

Relationships

Every business has established relationships with outside agencies, other companies, and individuals. These are non-contractual and can be simultaneously both ephemeral and extremely important to the enterprise.

Assembled Workforce.   One of the most obvious relationships of an enterprise is with its employees. It can be very costly to locate, hire, and train a workforce, as evidenced by the expenses incurred by companies to retain employees and reduce turnover. The more specialized the workforce the greater the cost of its assemblage and the larger its value to the enterprise.

Customer Relationships.   Every business has customers, but not every business has customer relationships in the sense referred to here. A newsstand in a large city probably has a number of customers who habitually purchase a daily newspaper, for example. Perhaps their walk from a bus stop to place of work takes them past the particular stand. There are probably other convenient locations to make the purchase, but whatever the reason they use this one. The newsstand proprietor does not know the identity of his customers or where they work and could not contact them to discover, for example, their interest in other publications. If the proprietor moved the newsstand to another location, it is not likely these customers would seek him out, rather they would patronize another stand better located to their route. This is not a customer relationship, in the sense used here.

Structure.   There is perhaps a pattern in the association between customer and business that might be described graphically as shown in Figure 7.1.

FIGURE 7.1   Value of Various Types of Customer Relationship

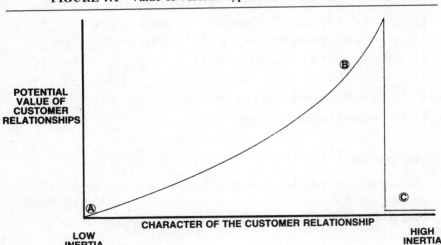

POTENTIAL
VALUE OF
CUSTOMER
RELATIONSHIPS

CHARACTER OF THE CUSTOMER RELATIONSHIP

LOW
INERTIA

HIGH
INERTIA

At Point A, there is no potentially valuable customer relationship, and the business can be characterized by:

1. Product(s) that are not exclusive, common, and easily obtained elsewhere.
2. No customer records.
3. Constant advertising to maintain sales.
4. Brand names are important.
5. Location is important.
6. Personality and skills of the owner/operator may be important.
7. Business activity may be seasonal.

Examples of businesses of this type are retail establishments such as a barbershop or beauty salon, a "trendy" cocktail lounge, a video rental store, deli, bakery, or the newsstand described above. One would expect sales to be very volatile and the possibility of business failure to be high. There is very little "inertia" to keep a customer in place.

At point C is a business monopoly. This could be a legal monopoly, such as a utility enterprise, or a business that has enough elements of exclusivity to make it a practical monopoly. An enterprise of this type would be characterized by:

1. Exclusive products or services, or ones that are sharply differentiated from competition.
2. Non-dependence on trademarks.
3. Little need for advertising.
4. Location unimportant.
5. Owner/operator personality and skills unimportant.

A water utility company would be an example of this type of business. It has both a legal monopoly and a practical one, in that it provides a service (water delivery) that is essential to life, has an exclusive franchise, and owns a distribution system that would be unfeasible for a competitor to duplicate. Sales and earnings of such an enterprise would be steady and the possibility of business failure would be low.

There is no separable customer relationship in this type of business. The association between customer and business exists because the business is the only purveyor of the required goods or services. The valuable asset in this type of business is the right (provided by franchise, usually) to the service territory, not that the business has developed stable customer relationships.

Therefore, no customer relationship exists at either extreme of the continuum.

For the businesses between these extremes, there exists some form of customer relationship that has been developed by advertising, good service, unique products, and the like. This relationship is something that would persist through a change of ownership, changes in personnel, and even a change in location. A business with the characteristics of the utility/monopoly (Point C) would be expected to have strong customer relationships, whereas one at the left side of the continuum would likely have weaker ones.

Identification.   For there to be a relationship as defined here, there should be some customer identifying records and/or some obligation or advantage on the part of either the business or customer to continue the relationship. These factors create some "inertia," which tends to maintain the relationship even when there is no contractual agreement between the parties, and are evidenced by:

1. Customer records that could be used in selling efforts.
2. Customer records that contain some history or useful information about the customer-business association: credit information; previous service; previous orders; specifications.
3. Customer prepayments for goods or services or long order lead time resulting in an order backlog.
4. Potential loss of discounts or privileges for discontinuing the relationship.
5. Costs or inconvenience associated with discontinuance, as when equipment is placed on customer premises.
6. Material selling costs associated with replacing the customer.

Types of Business.   Businesses in which an appraiser would expect to find significant customer relationships would include:

1. Professional practices, such as medical, dental, legal, accounting, financial planning, counselling.
2. Pharmacies (prescription records).
3. Publishers of periodicals (subscription list).

4. Providers of food service on customer premises.

5. Home health care providers.

6. Laboratories.

7. Advertising or public relations agencies.

8. Real estate or insurance agency.

9. Original equipment manufacturers for parts after-market (a "parts annuity" can exist where the manufacturer is the only supplier of parts).

10. Radio or television stations or newspapers (advertiser base).

11. Banks (core depositors).

12. Stock brokerages.

Distributor Relationships. A business that depends on others to distribute and/or sell its products may have established relationships of considerable value. Companies that sell cosmetics, cookware, and cleaning products in the residential market through representatives have no retail stores and the relationship with their representatives is extremely important. Other businesses may sell complex products in a highly technical market through "manufacturers representatives."

Although there may be a contract between the parties, it is usually one that can be terminated on short notice, and therefore does not itself insure a continuation of the relationship, though there would be turnover from other causes. Locating, hiring, training, and maintaining such representation can be a very costly process and, once accomplished, the relationship is an asset of value to the enterprise.

Unidentifiable

Although in recent years appraisers have analyzed, identified, and valued many intangible assets, there remains a residual, commonly referred to as "goodwill" and/or "going concern value." These two assets are combined by some, but there is reason to hold them separate and distinct.

Going Concern Value. Going concern value has been defined as "the additional element of value which attaches to property by reason of its existence as part of a going concern" (*VGS Corp.*, 68 T.C. 563, 569 [1977]).

Perhaps a somewhat bizarre example would serve better to describe going concern value. Suppose one were to assemble in a giant factory building all the tangible and intangible assets for a business:

1. Employees (first day on the job, wandering aimlessly).
2. Machinery (in crates).
3. Furniture and office machines (on the loading dock).
4. Computer and peripherals (boxed).
5. Cash (in bags).
6. Computer software (on disks and tape).
7. Office supplies (scattered about).

Obviously much must be done before this aggregation of assets is a business with an organization in place and a product ready for sale.

Across the street is an identical business that has a legal identity, has established relationships with financial, banking, legal, and accounting firms, has contracted with suppliers, designed a product, obtained an inventory, developed a business plan and an advertising program, written operating procedures and is poised and ready to go, *but has yet to make a sale* (so there can be no goodwill).

The difference between these two enterprises is going concern value (one business has the elements of a going concern in place). The measure of that value is the cost incurred to do all the organizing plus the profits lost during the process. One court has termed these two elements of going concern value "turnkey value" and "immediate use value" (*Miami Valley Broadcasting Corp. v. United States*, 499 F2d 677 [Ct. Cl. 1973]).

Goodwill.   Business people, attorneys, accountants, and judges have all had a try at defining this most intangible of intangibles.

Patronage.   Many equate goodwill with patronage, or the proclivity of customers to return to a business and recommend it to others. This situation results from superior service, personal relationships, advertising programs, and business policies that meet with favor in the marketplace.

Excess Earnings.   Another common aspect of a goodwill definition is the presence of "excess earnings." That is, a business that possesses significant goodwill is likely to have earnings that are greater than those required to provide a fair rate of return on the other assets of the business. Some even value a business enterprise this way, appraising the tangible assets and adding an amount for "goodwill," though this is not a technique subscribed to by appraisal professionals.

The relationship of excess earnings and the presence of goodwill has been thoroughly explored in the courts relative to utility rate cases. Here, again and again, it has been determined that a utility enterprise has no goodwill because its revenue requirement is set by regulation to provide an opportunity to earn a fair return only on its rate base (tangible assets and working capital). Therefore there are no excess earnings and no residual.

Residual. Another element in a redefinition of goodwill is that it represents the residual between the value of the enterprise as a whole and the value of the other identifiable assets. This is a permutation of the excess earnings concept, in that the value of the enterprise will only exceed the value of the identifiable assets (and create "room" for the residual) if there *are* excess earnings.

It is incorrect to depend entirely on one definition to the exclusion of the others. Can there be goodwill in a business that is losing money? Of course. A temporary escalation of expenses, a casualty loss, the opening of a new plant, or the development of a new product line can temporarily eliminate earnings, but goodwill can remain. Even over a longer period, persistent mismanagement can result in losses but both earning *capability* and goodwill can be present.

Can there be excess earnings and no goodwill? Certainly. Suppose a business has a single customer, locked in for several years under a lucrative contract. There might well be "excess earnings," but they are attributable to the contract, not goodwill. As another example, the local franchisee of a well-known company may have a very successful business with earnings in excess of those required to provide a fair return on other assets. It is entirely possible, however, that those "excess earnings" are attributable to the franchise and that the goodwill belongs to the franchising company.

Goodwill is a most elusive concept, and there is no one conclusive test for its presence or its magnitude.

VALUATION OF INTANGIBLE ASSETS

A valuation of intangible assets is nearly always for the purpose of estimating their fair market value. Therefore appraisers have the objective of measuring the economic benefits of ownership and use the now familiar three valuation methods: the market, cost, and income approaches. As with specific types of tangible assets, somewhat specialized techniques have been developed.

Market Approach

This approach is seldom used because, for the most part, intangible assets are so unique that sales of comparable property are not available to the appraiser. When sales of intangibles are made, it is usually a very non-public event between businesses and information is very difficult, if not impossible, to obtain. This technique is, however, appropriate in some circumstances.

There is an increasing variety of computer software packages on the market and this facilitates a market approach, though the degree of comparability must be carefully analyzed. One must be watchful of the amount of modification that must be done to suit a particular user, even for a package with flexible application.

One occasionally encounters industry standards that may appear to be valid market data but are often little more than "rules of thumb." These relate to exchange prices for property such as mortgage servicing rights, core deposits, subscribers, or certain types of license. These will not be repeated here because to do so would enhance their credibility.

The appraiser often uses market-derived data such as market rental rates, personnel search fees, or studies of salary ranges in valuations using the income approach. In general, however, this approach, as a stand-alone technique, has relatively little application for intangible assets.

Cost Approach

The cost approach is very useful to the appraiser for intangible assets, in that most intangible assets were created by past investment. Again, one must be careful not to apply a method blindly. The cost to obtain a liquor license several years ago may have been nominal, but the value today may be substantial because of market demand and short supply. The cost of obtaining a patent or copyright usually bears no relation to its value.

The appraiser will use either a *replacement cost* or a *trended cost* technique.

Replacement Cost. This technique involves the estimation of the cost to replace (as of the appraisal date) the intangible asset. On page 196 of the sample report in Chapter 10 is shown a replacement cost estimate for an assembled workforce. This estimate combines the costs that would be incurred to locate, hire, and train the appropriate classifications of employee. Use of the cost approach can be quite complex, such as when applied to the valuation of, for example, magazine subscribers or newspaper advertisers. This would include the estimation of the many costs that would be incurred in a sales campaign such as mailing list rentals, calls by salespersons, record creation and assumptions as to renewal rates, successful sales calls, and the like.

Trended Cost. When the appraiser's analysis reveals that historical costs are representative of the actual cost to create the asset at a previous time, the trended cost technique may be used. As described for tangible property, this involves the restatement of those historical costs to current levels, using an appropriate price trend.

Utilization. The cost approach is often utilized for:

1. Assembled workforce.
2. Advertising program.
3. Computer software.
4. Customer, subscriber list.
5. Designs, drawings.
6. Distributor network.
7. Going concern elements.
8. Government approvals, licenses.
9. Research and development.
10. Training materials.

Income Approach

Appraisers prefer this approach when it is appropriate. It requires three essential ingredients:

1. An income stream attributable to the asset.
2. The economic remaining life of the income stream.
3. A rate of return commensurate with the risk of realizing the income.

Income Stream

Directly Attributable. In some situations the income attributable to an intangible asset is obtainable directly, such as from a contractual agreement. Examples are: a copyright royalty, a patent license fee, a franchise fee.

Even in these examples, the appraiser is not "home free" because, while the contract defines how the income is determined (such as a percentage of sales), the appraiser must still estimate future sales to calculate the potential income stream.

Indirectly Attributable. In most cases, the appraiser must develop an estimate of potential income for an intangible asset. This analysis usually begins with the subject company's income statement.

For example, in an appraisal which includes the customer base of a lawn-care company, the appraiser would first examine the current financial statements. The company might record revenues from several sources: residential service, commercial service, and one-time services. At any particular time, the revenues represent the cumulative sales to all customers since the last income statement, *not* necessarily the customers that exist at the appraisal date. In addition, the appraiser is interested in the ongoing income, not that derived from one-time services that may never occur again. Recorded revenues must therefore be adjusted to reflect the revenue that could be expected from the customer base at the appraisal date.

Similarly, the recorded expenses may reflect non-recurring items as well as elements that are not relevant in an appraisal. The appraiser would apply accounting principles to match expenses with the revenues of the customer base and would typically exclude expenses for:

1. Advertising to obtain new customers.
2. Selling and marketing.
3. Research and development.
4. Opening a new plant.
5. Acquiring a company.
6. Legal expenses.
7. Corporate overheads.
8. Financing, treasury functions.
9. Recruiting.

The appraiser is always concerned with "capturing" a specific population (in this case customers as of the appraisal date) and determining the income-producing capability of *that* population. This is always going to be a "dying" population that in time will be gone, along with its income. The appraiser will look at this as a stand-alone business and capture only the expenses necessary to adminster the declining population and receive the revenues.

In many cases, the financial statements do not contain *any* relevant data and the appraiser must utilize other methods: "relief from royalty," premium price, and expense reduction.

Relief from Royalty. This technique is based on the assumption that the owner of an intangible asset such as a patent, copyright, trade secret, or trademark "escapes" from payment of a royalty by virtue of that ownership. The earnings in the business segments affected by that intangible are greater thereby, and the increase in earnings is measured by an appropriate royalty rate. Stated another way, the owner has the opportunity to license the intangible and enjoy royalty revenues in addition to the earnings from his or her own business.

The determination of an appropriate royalty rate when there is no licensing experience in the subject company has been one of the most difficult appraisal tasks. The licensing of intangible assets is a very proprietary matter and royalties are not made public. An analysis of this has led to the development of several criteria here incorporated into a system to assist in this quantification. These include:

1. Market share (e.g., an intangible asset associated with a product that enjoys a large market share would command a royalty at the high end of the range).
2. Recognition.
3. Market size.
4. Profitability.
5. Market growth.
6. Competition.
7. Barriers to market entry.
8. Product life.
9. Alternative markets (uses).
10. Brand loyalty.

In the final analysis, the estimation of an appropriate royalty rate may be largely subjective, but an experienced appraiser will have some benchmarks and logic supporting a conclusion.

Premium Price.   This technique, often used for trademarks, is based on the fact that a product with a known trademark will command a higher price in the market than will an identical product without the trademark. This price premium is a measure of the income-producing capability of the trademark. An appraiser will investigate whether a manufacturer is selling a product with a "name brand" or with a "house brand." The difference in price may be attributable to the trademark.

This general idea has been used to establish the value of contracts for sports or entertainment figures. If ballpark attendance is measurably greater when "Slugger Sam" is in the lineup or if ticket prices are higher when the main event features "K. O. Nelson," there is a measure of value.

Premium pricing can be used in an income valuation of a patent as well. An example would be a patented feature on a product that is otherwise the same as others on the market. If this feature makes the patent owner's product more desirable, then it is likely to carry a premium price.

Expense Reduction.   This technique, often used by the appraiser in valuing patents or trade secrets, is based on the fact that a patent or proprietary know-how can enable a company to reduce costs of production. This cost reduction could come about by increasing output speed, reducing waste, utilizing less expensive materials, cutting power costs, and the like. A cost reduction increases earnings and is a measure of the income attributable to the asset.

This technique can also be used when the expense "reduction" is a measure of an advantageous contract such as a lease or financing at lower than market rates or a supply contract at terms more favorable than could be obtained in the market at the time of the appraisal.

Economic Remaining Life.   Since the valuation objective is to estimate the present value of future economic benefits, the *duration* and *pattern* of the income stream are essential elements.

Duration.   The length of time that income can be expected to flow from an intangible asset is a function of many conditions. It can depend on the statutory effectiveness of a patent or copyright or upon the terms of a contract.

Most often, however, the economic life of the income stream depends on factors outside of the law or the terms of an agreement.

Even when there is some legal basis for the duration of an income stream, it may not be determinative. One of the most unpredictable incomes is that associated with the copyright of music. A composer writes the score for a moving picture. The movie is successful, and royalties are received during the year or two that the picture is shown in theaters and on television. For a period of years the income may be minimal. It is not inconceivable that suddenly the music is selected as the background for a radio and television commercial and royalty income is higher than ever. In the same unpredictable way the literary works of an author can spring into popularity, or be utilized in a moving picture, or become the basis for a television series.

Most often, the income associated with rights to intangible assets is related to a product and the income is dependent on sales of the product. The appraiser must therefore be concerned with market share, competition, price, and marketing strategy.

Pattern. It may not be enough to develop an estimate of remaining life if the amount of income will vary significantly during that period. The present value of future income is sensitive to both the amount of income and its timing. Most products go through a cycle of introduction, growth, maturity, and decline. The appraiser must be sensitive to the age of the related product.

Even where there is no "product," the pattern of income can vary sharply. The income from a portfolio of residential mortgages will decline over time as mortgages are paid. A typical home mortgage has an economic life of eight to ten years in spite of its 25-year contractual term. An appraisal of such a portfolio, using a capitalization of income approach, must recognize this reality.

Chapter 8 provides a more complete discussion of how the appraiser analyzes both the duration and pattern of economic life.

Rate of Return. The final ingredient in the income approach is the determination of an appropriate rate of return to use in the capitalization process. Chapter 5 discussed the means to calculate a rate of return, or discount rate. That discussion related to the determination of a rate appropriate for an entire business enterprise.

Variability. All of the individual assets of an enterprise do not have the same investment risk. The rate of return for a business represents the composite rate for all the assets in the business, some which have lower and some which have higher risk. Russell L. Parr aptly ascribes this risk difference to "transferability, liquidity, and asset versatility."

Working Capital.   An investment in the net working capital component of the enterprise would typically represent the lowest risk because it represents assets that are liquid and very "versatile" in that they can be redeployed relatively easily.

Tangible Assets.   Tangible assets are less liquid but can usually be separated from the enterprise. They represent the middle of the risk range.

Intangible Assets.   An appraiser recognizes that an investment in the intangible assets of an enterprise is at greater risk because these assets are usually inseparable from the business and have little value outside of it. Their value is also subject to great change due to factors beyond the control of the managers of the business.

Determination.   The starting point is therefore a determination of an appropriate rate of return for the enterprise as a whole. From that benchmark the appraiser estimates rates of return for the component investments in the business "portfolio." The confirmation is that the average of the individual rates of return, weighted by the asset values, is commensurate with that judged to be correct for the enterprise.

Value Calculation.   Calculating the value of an individual intangible asset by the income approach is the same as for a business enterprise, as described in Chapter 5.

A capitalization in perpetuity would be appropriate for *trademarks, copyrights,* and *goodwill*.

When the intangible asset is judged to have a limited life, value as measured by an income approach should give consideration to the tax benefits of amortization (capital recovery). When applied to an entire business, capital recovery is reflected in depreciation expense. When this technique is used for an individual intangible asset, some recognition must be given to the fact that it will be amortizable for income tax purposes. The reduction in effective income tax rate because of the deductability of the amortization is an additional economic benefit to the acquirer. The value of the asset then becomes: (1) The present worth of the income attributable to the asset, plus (2) the present worth of the tax saving provided by amortization.

FIGURE 7.2 Checklist of Common Intangible Assets

INTANGIBLE ASSETS	METHOD OF VALUATION	AMORTIZATION
Patents	Income or Cost	Yes
Software	Cost or Market	Yes
Licenses	Income	Yes
Copyrights	Income	Yes
Favorable Contracts:		
Space	Income	Yes
Raw Material	Income	Yes
Distribution	Income	Yes
Financing	Income	Yes
Services	Income	Yes
Insurance	Income	Yes
Customer Base	Cost or Income	Perhaps
Formulas	Cost or Income	Perhaps
Proprietary Know-how	Cost or Income	Perhaps
Assembled Workforce	Cost	Perhaps
Research and Development	Cost	Perhaps
Advertising Programs	Cost	Perhaps
Training Materials	Cost	Perhaps
Trademarks	Cost or Income	No
Tradenames	Cost or Income	No
Goodwill	Income	No

This is expressed in a formula (known to many as the "patent formula"):

$$V = (RS \times PWF1) + (V/L \times T \times PWF2)$$

where

V = value.
RS = royalty savings or other income attributable to the asset.
$PWF1$ = present worth factor for the appropriate rate and number of periods of economic remaining life.

PWF2 = present worth factor applicable to the tax savings, which is often judged to be at a lower rate than for the base income.
L = economic remaining life.
T = income tax rate.

Utilization.   Figure 7.2 presents a checklist of the more common intangible assets together with the valuation method most appropriate for each and an indication of the likelihood of developing support for taxable amortization.

REFERENCE

1. Financial Accounting Standards Board, "Statement of Financial Accounting Concepts No. 6," 1985, p. 62.

8

ESTIMATING ECONOMIC LIFE

The economic life of property is of interest to business management, the engineering and accounting professions, financial institutions, the insurance industry, and government. The concept of economic life is also an integral part of the appraisal process. Chapter 4 pointed out that value is represented by the future benefits of ownership compressed into a single payment. Knowing the expected duration of those economic benefits is essential to quantifying them. This concept was touched upon in discussing the measurement of depreciation in the cost approach and in describing the requirement, when using the income approach, of estimating the duration and pattern of the income stream.

ECONOMIC LIFE DEFINED

Economic life could be described as the period during which it is profitable to use an asset. Economic life ends when it is no longer profitable to use an asset (the future benefits are used up) or when it is more profitable to use another asset. The *service life* of an asset is the period from its installation to the date of its retirement, irrespective of its earning capability along the way. Service life and economic life do not necessarily coincide.

Legislated Lives

For years, schedules of suggested or required lives for depreciation have been a part of the federal income tax code. At the beginning, these were realistic estimates of typical economic life and became part of tax legislation in order to reduce controversy between the government and taxpayers. Legislators soon realized, however, that changing these lives (and depreciation methods as well) was a relatively easy way to alter corporate tax rates and to attempt to manage the economy. Property lives for tax depreciation have therefore been in almost continual change, with the result that they bear little resemblance to realistic economic life.

Legal/Contractual Life

The economic life of tangible assets is commonly not affected by legal or contract terms. These assets belong to the business and remain in place as long as the management of the business wants.

Many intangible assets do have a recognized legal or contractual life. For example:

1. Patents.
2. Copyrights.
3. Leases.
4. Supply or distribution contracts.
5. Subscriptions.
6. Mortgages or other loan agreements.
7. License agreements.

An appraiser analyzes these situations to determine whether the legal or contract terms are controlling with respect to remaining economic life. In many cases, economic life is shorter than legal life. The effectiveness of a patent may end before its 17-year life because of advancing technology or because the product in which it is used has lost its place in the market. On the other hand, the economic life of a magazine subscription may be longer than its contract life if there is a history of renewals. In most cases, the legal or contractual life is *not* controlling with respect to economic life. The appraiser must therefore embark on an independent analysis. This is not entirely a subjective process, however, as the following sections of this chapter will present.

ECONOMIC LIFE, CAPITAL RECOVERY, AND VALUE

Because of the close relationship of value and economic life, appraisers are often consulted regarding the economic remaining life of assets. In this area there is a community of interest among accountants, appraisers, and business managers.

Capital Recovery

When a manager of a business or an accountant decides that an expenditure is an asset (see the FASB quote at the beginning of Chapter 7), recovery of that expenditure (depreciation) must begin and continue as long as that expenditure *is* an asset (as long as there are future economic benefits).

When an asset is retired prematurely (vis à vis the capital recovery period), a loss occurs, equal to the unrecovered cost. When the service life is longer than the capital recovery period, the business enjoys earnings greater than it otherwise would during the extended period. In either case, there is a mis-matching of the revenues generated by the asset and the cost of ownership. For a business with many assets, the impact is usually not significant when the pluses and minuses are offset, but an important accounting objective has not been met, nevertheless.

A realistic economic life, giving consideration to all the factors that cause property retirement, should be the basis for establishing capital recovery periods.

Regulated Industries.   One area in which there has been extensive scrutiny of capital recovery is for regulated utility companies. These are very capital-intensive enterprises and therefore depreciation expense is a significant cost of doing business. In addition, accumulated depreciation affects the rate base upon which rates for the future will be set. These are both costs that must be borne by current and future ratepayers. Regulatory authorities, therefore, have been very attentive to capital recovery rates which are based on estimations of economic life.

This attention began in 1909 when the Supreme Court decided *Knoxville v. Knoxville Water Company* (212 U.S. 1) and discussed annual and accrued depreciation and its importance in regulation. Since then it has been the objective of utility managers and regulators to reflect accurately depreciation expense and to have the capital recovery period and economic life be the same (to avoid under- and over-recoveries). Therefore there has been a great amount of effort to develop reliable methods for estimating the economic life of property.

The analysis techniques that have come from this effort have been of considerable assistance to appraisal practitioners.

Value

Since value is also measured by future economic benefits, the net book value (cost less accumulated depreciation) *ought* to mirror the decline in value. Stated another way, when the value of an asset is zero (no future economic benefits of ownership), it should cease being an asset on the balance sheet (cost equal to the accumulated depreciation).

Thus, under ideal conditions, the capital recovery period, service life, and economic life ought to be identical. In actuality this is a rare occasion indeed. The primary reason for this lack of success is that conditions change and what appeared at the time of investment to be an asset with a 10-year life turned out to be scrap after five years or was still going strong after 20.

Appraisers and accountants have therefore had a common interest in advancing techniques that would assist them in the analysis of the economic life of property.

ESTIMATING ECONOMIC LIFE

Background

In 1935, the then Iowa Engineering Experiment Station (of Iowa State University) published Bulletin 125, *Statistical Analyses of Industrial Property Retirements*, which is regarded by many as the seminal work of this field. In the 1967 edition, Harold A. Cowles wrote:

> By observation and classification of the ages at death of hundreds of thousands of people, actuaries have built up mortality tables by which the average life of humans and the expectancy of life at any age can be determined accurately. Similarly, engineers and industrial statisticians have assembled the life histories and ages at retirement of many types of industrial property units from which they are enabled to forecast the probable lives of similar units still remaining in service. The estimate of life expectancy for a single unit or a small group of units may be in considerable error. However, the probability of error is reduced when the service conditions of the property are taken into consideration and evaluated by engineers of expert judgement in these matters, the estimate being revised from time to time as the life history of the property unfolds.[1]

One result of that analysis has been to provide a number of techniques that can be utilized in the determination of the economic life of assets. All of these techniques have a common basis, however:

The estimation of expected remaining service lives of industrial property has always been and will continue to be based upon the considered judgment of the engineer or the technically competent estimator. Judgment is exercised through a consideration of what is known about the past and the present life characteristics, and how they will be influenced by expected future conditions. It is significant to note that the starting point of the estimation is knowledge of past experience.[2]

Studies of Historical Life

Bulletin 125 describes six methods for determining average life, five of which begin with the construction of survivor curves from historical retirement data and one which calculates average life directly.

Turnover Method. This method requires that one know the annual additions and retirements of property. The age of the retirements is not known, only the year in which they occurred. When data are available for a long period and when the property is stable, this method produces acceptable results. It is not a reliable method for new and growing properties or for changing conditions.

Survivor Curve Methods. The remaining methods for analyzing retirement data result in the development of a survivor curve, which graphically depicts the duration and pattern of life expectancy for a group of property units. The ordinate to the curve indicates the percentage (or number) of the original group surviving. The abscissa indicates the passage of time. Figure 8.1 shows a typical survivor curve.

Such a curve is at times referred to as a "mortality curve," but the originators of the concept prefer "survivor curve" to differentiate their studies from those of human life, though the underlying principles are the same.

Some additional explanation relative to Figure 8.1 might assist in its understanding:

1. The survivor curve itself is a "reverse S" shape that, in this case, illustrates that at the beginning of life retirements are few. As age increases, retirements become more frequent (the curve slopes more steeply). Toward the end of life retirements are again less frequent. If one were to plot the frequency of retirements, a bell-shaped curve would result.

2. The total area under the curve represents the amount of service that would be rendered by the property units during their life.

3. The average service life is the area under the curve (percent-years) divided by 100 percent. In Figure 8.1 this is the distance "A," or 10 years, for the group at age zero. At any other time-point, the horizontal distance between the survivor and remaining life curves is the remaining life (shown as distance "C").

4. For a group of property units with an age of 16 years (shown at distance "B"), the remaining service is represented by the shaded area.

5. One should note that there can be a significant difference between *average* service life and *maximum* life. In Figure 8.1, at age zero, the average life expectancy is 10 years, though it will be 30 years until the last unit is retired.

The survivor curve represents both the duration and pattern of service life for a group of property units. It is derived from historical retirement data. Appraisers recognize, however, that the amount and type of historical data vary considerably. Therefore several techniques are available whose use depends on the quantity and nature of the information available.

Individual-Unit Method. This technique is used when the data indicate only the number of property units retired during a year, or for several years, together with their age at retirement. The survivor curve derived from these data is based only on the experience of retired property and does not give weight to the property units still in service, which is one of the disadvantages of this technique.

Original-Group Method. This technique follows a group of property units placed in service in a common year, noting those that survive at successive later years. The curve will reach zero only if all the original group are retired during the time span studied, and is an accurate representation of the life characteristics of the particular group, but may not be representative of other vintage groups.

Composite Original-Group Method. More than one group can be combined into a single group and plotted as for the original-group method described above. This combines the experience of several groups as one and is best used when successive-year vintage groups are used. For example, com-

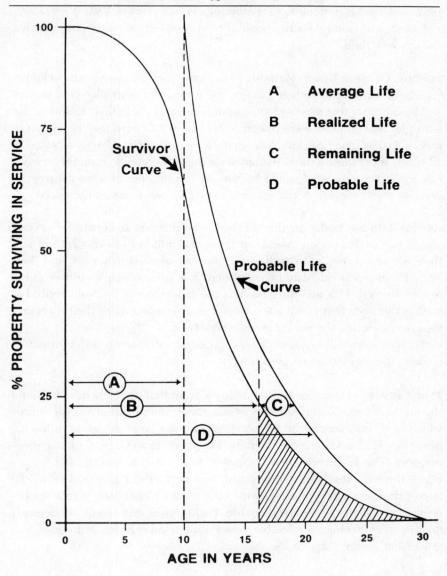

FIGURE 8.1 Typical Survivor Curve

A   Average Life
B   Realized Life
C   Remaining Life
D   Probable Life

Survivor Curve

Probable Life Curve

% PROPERTY SURVIVING IN SERVICE

AGE IN YEARS

bining the experience of property groups placed in service in 1980, 1981, 1982, and 1983 is preferable to combining vintage years of 1920, 1940, 1960, and 1980, and minimizes the possibility of masking mortality patterns that change over time.

Multiple Original-Group Method.   Using this method, one needs to know, for a large number of vintage groups, the number of units placed in service and the number that survived at one point subsequent to that. Knowing, for example, that 50 units were placed in service in 1970 and that 10 remain in service in 1987, one can conclude that 20 percent survived after a period of 17 years. If the same data were known for the 1971 vintage, then the survival rate for a 16-year period would be known. Continuing, one can construct a survivor curve with each vintage year providing one point on the curve.

Annual-Rate Method.   In this method, observations are made for several years. For each year one needs to know the number of units retired and their age at retirement as well as the number of units in service and their ages. From this is calculated a retirement rate from which a survivor curve can be derived. This method considers the experience of the units retired as well as the units that survive and provides a clear picture of the retirement experience during the period of years observed.

An appraiser will often study several bands of years in order to detect shifts in life characteristics over time.

Type Curves.   From the studies at Iowa State that developed and refined the methodologies described above came the development of 18 type curves which best represented the life behavior of many large groups of industrial property. The curves have come to be known as "Iowa Curves" among practitioners. The 18 curves were designated $L_0 \ldots L_5$, $S_0 \ldots S_5$, and $R_0 \ldots R_5$, to denote left-modal, symmetrical, and right-modal shapes. Left-modal curves describe a life pattern in which the greatest frequency of retirements occurs prior to the average service life. Right-modal retirement frequency is greatest after average service life, and symmetrical retirement frequency is greatest at average service life.

Simulated Plant Balance Method.   This is a computerized method of analyzing retirement experience that requires only a series of plant balances (quantity of units or dollars invested at a point in time) and the number of units added or retired in the intervals between the balances. The system uses type curves such as the Iowa Curves and successively compares the experience they generate with the actual balances to determine the curve with the "best fit." This method is less precise than developing a survivor curve from specific experience, but it is useful when detailed retirement data are not available.

Forecast or Life Span Method.   This method is useful for properties that are an aggregation of many individual assets, each of which may have a different life characteristic. Examples would be: building structures; electric power plants; process equipment, such as an individual product plant within a refinery or petrochemical facility.

When it is desirable to express an opinion about the remaining life of the whole property rather than its component parts, the life span method can be used. A judgment is made relative to the components' remaining life, considering their normal life, their age, and their relationship to the other components. The component lives are weighted together to form a conclusion about the remaining life of the whole property. As an example, the heating system in an office building has a normal life of 15 years. The building structure has a normal life of 50 years. For a new building, the remaining life could be estimated by weighting together these two investments and their respective remaining lives to conclude a composite remaining life of, say, 48 years. If, however, the building is already 45 years old and has a new heating system, the remaining life of both is 5 years because the life of the structure is controlling.

These are oversimplified examples but serve to convey the underlying theory of this method.

Subjective Elements

Estimation of the remaining economic life of tangible or intangible assets is not even close to being an exact science, in spite of the implications of precision contained in descriptions above. These analysis techniques can only deal with historical data, and they are at their best when:

1.   Complete and accurate data are available about past additions and retirements of property.
2.   They are applied to the study of relatively large numbers of similar assets, such as telephone poles or a fleet of trucks.

3. Historical experience is an appropriate guide for the future.

4. Considerable history is available, such as a complete life cycle.

These are the reasons why these methods are in routine use in the estimation of economic remaining life for utility property, where detailed property records are the norm and the types of property are appropriate.

When Data Is Unavailable. Outside of the utility business segment, the application of these techniques becomes more difficult for the appraiser. Most businesses have no reason to keep a record of assets retired several years ago, whether they were machines, customers, subscribers, employees, or advertisers. With computerized accounting systems, subscribers who cancel, for example, are most likely simply dropped from the system. There is no business reason to maintain such a record.

An important part of the appraiser's assignment, therefore, may consist of investigating the types of records that *are* kept in order to decide whether any of these techniques are feasible. This is a worthwhile investigation, because the second, third, and fourth try sometimes uncovers a source of information in an unlikely area. To use these techniques, an appraiser must be creative and persistent. Often only a few years' experience is available, either because the data are incomplete or because the company or product is new. The survivor curve is therefore very short and must be extended mathematically or by the use of type curves.

Combining Data. Often the appraiser must combine data from more than one source in order to form a conclusion. For example, an appraiser is engaged to value the depositors in a bank. One group is the customers holding certificates of deposit. In analyzing their turnover, it is observed that the holders of short-term CDs nearly always rolled them over at maturity. This leads to a further look and the discovery that nearly all of these customers also have checking accounts into which the interest from the CDs is being deposited. A study had already been made of the remaining life of checking account holders and therefore these data could be used to forecast the probable remaining life of the CD accounts after maturity.

In other examples, data relative to the failure rate for small business could be utilized to estimate the life of newspaper advertisers in a suburban area or the population turnover and home mortgage life experience could be used to augment sparse data on the turnover in the newspaper's subscriber base.

Change Is Everywhere. One would think that the recipe for a food product or the formula for a paint pigment or metal alloy would be long-lived information. In actuality, formulas such as these are constantly changing because of the availability of raw materials; changes in the quality or specifications of raw materials; changes in taste and preference (e.g., low-sodium, low-fat, low-sugar foods); efforts to obtain less costly materials; environmental concerns (e.g., lead and petroleum distillates in paint); and changes in marketing (e.g., longer shelf life required).

The result is that a formula for white paint or a recipe for cupcakes may have been modified many times, even though the product line has been in existence for many years. Computer software is a classic example of this situation. Almost every business has a computer program for processing the payroll and has had one for several years. Is it the same software today that it was five years ago? Almost certainly not. Small but continual modifications have been made.

Higher and Higher Tech. One of the most difficult estimates of economic life concerns assets related to new technology. An example would be the tangible and intangible assets in an enterprise that began two years ago to develop a product which is, at the time of the appraisal, six months from being introduced to the market. Millions of dollars may have been spent during the development period and the appraiser must decide how many of them now constitute assets of material value, *and* what is their economic remaining life. Here, specific history is non-existent and the future is uncertain. In this situation the appraiser must ask questions such as:

1. What is the potential market?
2. Who are the competitors?
3. What will the further development costs be?
4. What product or service is being replaced?
5. Are financial resources present to see the project through?
6. What is the level of protection (patents, trade secrets, head start)?
7. What is the cost of market entry?

It is a challenge to work on such an assignment, and it is easy to become caught up in the ever-faster pace of technological development. But one must not, however, become too enamored of this pace and forget that there *are* electric typewriters out there that are 15 years old and perfect for what they are being used for and will last another 10 years. There are third-generation computers and second-generation telephone switching equipment doing very well in their present use.

Generation Gap.   One tool is to trace the development of a product or service through its "generations" to detect whether there is a constant progression or, more typically, an increasingly shorter generation life span.

A good example is computer hardware, which has moved through several generations from vacuum tubes and unit record peripherals (punched cards), to transistors, to chips and floppy disks. Another example is the well-documented progression in communications equipment from manual switchboards to digital switches. Medical diagnostic equipment has undergone similar "generational" changes that can be tracked.

This type of analysis provides the appraiser with an overview of how fast technological advances are taking place in the subject industry. It also gives some insight as to whether these advances come in evolutionary fashion or in "breakthroughs."

Outside Influences.   It seems that forces external to a business are exerting ever-increasing influence over managers and the business assets that they use. The value and economic life of a loan or mortgage portfolio held by a financial institution can vary substantially with the vagaries of the interest rate. The value of an inventory fluctuates with the trading value of currency. A chemical process or material that is a basic product building block today is restricted in the marketplace tomorrow. Employee turnover may be significantly changed as a result of legislation. Changes in health or safety standards can render a process, product, or service too costly to compete. The impact of product liability is well known.

The purpose of mentioning these facts is not to inject a political philosophy but to underline the myriad factors that must be considered by the appraiser in coming to a conclusion about the economic remaining life of business property.

Summary

The techniques and factors to be considered in estimating economic remaining life could be the subject of several chapters. This discussion is, however, not to make the reader expert in life estimation, but rather to present an overview of this subject from the appraiser's point of view and to emphasize that:

1. Estimating economic remaining life is an integral part of the appraisal process.

2. The appraiser's objectives are the same as those of business managers and accountants.

3. The process is not just a completely subjective exercise.

4. There are quantitative tools available.

5. There are times when these tools should be used, and times when they are inappropriate.

REFERENCES

1. Robley Winfrey, *Statistical Analyses of Industrial Property Retirements*. Ames: Engineering Research Institute, Iowa State University, 1967, p. 1.

2. Ibid., p. 2.

9

PUTTING IT ALL TOGETHER

THE FINAL APPRAISAL TASK

At the beginning of Chapter 1 were outlined the steps required to complete an appraisal: (1) project definition and planning, (2) investigation, (3) analysis, and (4) reporting.

Steps 2 and 3 involve obtaining property descriptions, field inventories, pricing, market surveys, financial analysis, and reaching a value conclusion. One can easily imagine, in an appraisal of the tangible and intangible assets of a business enterprise, how many times and on how many levels the investigation and analysis steps are being taken.

As an example, these tasks must be accomplished for each machine, each building, and each land parcel that comprise a plant. They are addressed again for each plant in a division and for each division and, ultimately, for the entire enterprise. For each economic entity, consideration must be made relative to economic obsolescence and again at higher levels and again for the business as a whole.

Toward the end of building this pyramid of value representing the entire enterprise, the appraiser must test the fit of the individual blocks and, where needed, smooth them. In practice, this is an iterative process, which is fancy language for "trial and error"—not haphazard, but a reflection of the many variables that must be considered and that the process does not lend itself to a formula approach.

Correlation/Reconciliation

The process of smoothing the blocks is called by some "correlation," by others "reconciliation," and by all, difficult. It can perhaps be best described in an example.

Earlier it was noted that appraisers of business assets tend to be specialists. Assume that, in the valuation of a business, three appraisers are given the assignment: a real estate appraiser, a machinery appraiser, and an intangible asset appraiser. Each goes to the various plant locations of the company and completes the assignment. They meet back at their office and assemble their conclusions of value for each of the many classifications of property and for each plant location. When all the values are totaled, they equal $10 million. Is that the correct value of the assets of this business? Perhaps. There is a piece of the puzzle missing.

While the plant appraising has been going on, a fourth member of the team, the business appraiser, has been analyzing financial statements, interviewing engineering, marketing, and production staff, and studying the performance of comparable companies and investments and has concluded values for the whole enterprise, as well as some divisions (economic entities). The business appraiser has concluded an enterprise value of $9 million as the maximum amount supportable by the earnings capability of the enterprise. What to do?

To those readers who read Chapter 4 carefully, it would appear that there is economic obsolescence of $1 million. Where does it belong? Thus begins the correlation process. It requires a team effort for all the appraisers to re-examine their conclusions in the light of the economics of the operation(s). Perhaps the business appraiser made a mistake. Perhaps the intangibles appraiser capitalized more income than the whole enterprise can produce. Perhaps there are certain plants that were valued too high because they are making a product in decline. Perhaps the value of all the plants in a given division must be penalized because of the low prospective earnings of that group alone. Perhaps the conclusion is reached that the $1 million is truly economic obsolescence and applies to all the assets of the enterprise. But should it, in fact, be applied equally to all?:

Land that was valued as if vacant and available can not logically be given an economic penalty, because its value is not dependent on specific industry economics.

Machinery and equipment may be reduced, but what if it is general purpose and readily marketable? The potential reduction in that case is probably low, because it should not be lower than orderly liquidation value. Very special purpose equipment may provide more room for adjustment because its use outside of the enterprise is limited.

Intangible assets should be examined carefully. First, their value is more difficult to ascertain and there is more likelihood for error. Second, they are first to suffer loss in value when the economics of the business decline.

One can easily see why it may require many iterations before a conclusion is reached that is acceptable to all the appraiser participants. A similar exercise would result if the business appraiser had concluded $12 million.

The Appraisal Team.   The above example is highly over-simplified in order to illustrate the process. A fifth member of the team, the engagement manager, would have insured that there was proper communication within the team so that each appraiser knew what the others were finding as their individual analysis unfolded. Professional appraisers do not "put blinders on" and work as individuals on an assignment such as this because they understand the relationship of asset and business enterprise values.

The business appraiser is dependent on the real estate and equipment appraisers to provide detailed knowledge about plant operations, quality of underlying assets, and the need for future construction. The business and intangible asset appraisers must work closely together, using the same financial data. In practice, business enterprise and intangible assets are handled by the same individual. The real estate and equipment appraisers should have foreknowledge about the general direction of enterprise value so that consideration can be included as they proceed.

Single Asset Appraisals.   Even when the appraisal assignment involves only a specific asset, such as real estate, a piece of machinery, or an advantageous contract, this process of correlation will occur. The consideration of economic obsolescence may not be present, as in the example above, but the appraiser will have values developed by the cost, market, and income approaches to reconcile.

Throughout, this book has referred to the *indications* of value produced by the cost, market, and income approaches. These are only *indications* of not conclusions of value because they have not been examined to determine the weight that should be given to each in the conclusion. Therefore, there is need for correlation no matter what the size of the appraisal assignment.

It is a rare occasion, indeed, when a value can be concluded on the basis of a single approach and calculation. Appraisers just don't find pyramids already shaped and ready to present to clients. Even the smallest of them must be built and trued.

SUMMARY

The purpose of this book has been to provide some assistance, from an appraiser's perspective, to managers in business and government and to other professionals who might require valuation services. The appraisal profession was described and some thoughts on how to select and work with an appraiser and how to recognize the need for valuation services were presented. The appraisal procedure was explained for two reasons: (1) the appraisal process is little understood outside of the profession; and (2) an understanding of the appraisal process will greatly assist clients in finding, selecting, and working with an appraiser. This in turn will ensure a successful valuation for both client and appraiser. The following paragraphs summarize the essence of the chapter discussions.

Chapter 1. There is a wide range of specialization available within the profession, and a body of ethical practices that is common to the various professional societies and the appraisal disciplines.

Chapter 2. Carefully selecting an appraiser is the first step toward a successful engagement, and special attention should be given to matching the appraiser and the particular assignment. On a large engagement, especially, a client should be prepared to participate in both planning and execution.

Chapter 3. Appraisal services can be utilized to good advantage in a large number of business situations. Many of these situations pass by unnoticed because the business manager does not know the range of appraisal disciplines or cannot foresee the need to have an appraisal ready for future events.

Chapter 4. An appraiser does not depend on unsupported guesswork. There are time-tested methods available that have their roots in economic theory.

Chapter 5. An appraiser views a business enterprise as an aggregation of myriad individual assets that can be identified and valued. There is a difference between valuing a business enterprise and the securities of a business enterprise.

Chapter 6.   Appraising tangible assets can be a very labor-intensive (and expensive) undertaking. Several techniques are used to value tangible assets, and these should be carefully matched against the type of property and the appraisal objective.

Chapter 7.   A large number of business intangible assets can be identified and valued. As we continue to develop into a service economy, these assets will become ever more important to business managers and transactions involving them will become more frequent.

Chapter 8.   Estimating economic life is an integral part of valuation and there are well-established techniques available to the appraiser.

Chapter 10.   An appraisal report is not simply a letter stating an opinion. Although a value conclusion is an opinion, it must be supported logically, with facts, and with a quantitative analysis.

10

THE APPRAISAL REPORT

As noted in the first chapter, the appraisal report may be the sole contact with the appraisal process for management within the client organization as well as outside agencies. Therefore it is very important that it be complete, clear, and contain all of the necessary documentation of the appraiser's analysis and conclusions.

This chapter presents a sample appraisal report, annotated to highlight its essential parts to give the reader, as potential client, a basis for evaluating the product of an appraisal professional.

There are various forms of appraisal report, ranging from a two- or three-page letter to a multi-volume work, and the difference is usually dictated by the size and complexity of the property appraised. There are, however, certain essential ingredients. These are illustrated with a report comprised of a transmittal letter that is an executive summary and a narrative report that provides additional detail. Note: Author's comments are italicized throughout.

TRANSMITTAL LETTER/EXECUTIVE SUMMARY

Acme, Inc.
Moorestown, New Jersey

Gentlemen:

We have completed a valuation of the tangible and intangible assets associated with the business enterprise known as the ABC Company ("ABC" or "the Company"), whose corporate offices are located in Mount Laurel, New Jersey. The purpose of this valuation is to express our opinion of the fair market value of all tangible and intangible assets as of January 1, 1987, so as to provide a basis, for financial reporting and income tax purposes, to allocate the purchase price to the assets acquired.

> *The transmittal letter is addressed to the client and sets forth the assets appraised, the "as of" date, the premise of value, and the understood purpose of the appraisal.*

When the term "fair market value" is used in this report, it is defined as the amount at which the property would exchange between a willing buyer and seller, neither being compelled to act, each having knowledge of all relevant facts, with equity to both, and with the assumption that the facilities will remain at their present location for the continuation of current operations.

> *The premise of value is defined.*

In formulating our conclusions of value for these assets as part of a going concern, we have reviewed balance sheets, income statements, and other financial statistics which we requested and which were furnished by the company and which we accepted as properly representative of business operations and conditions. Principal company locations were inspected and our investigation included interviews with company management.

> *This briefly explains what the appraiser had available and the extent of the analysis. If the appraiser had less than full access to the property or had to make assumptions about unknown conditions, it would be noted here.*

Based upon our review of these data, and after providing for adequate working capital in addition to the values of the assets appraised, it is our conclusion that the prospective profits are sufficient to support an arm's-length exchange between a willing buyer and seller at the appraised fair market value.

> *The appraiser explains that a financial review was done and that he or she is satisfied that the business is viable and that there will be earnings to support the values concluded.*

This valuation report includes:

This executive summary, which briefly describes the property, the nature and scope of our valuation analysis, and presents the conclusion of value for the assets identified.

A report which details the purpose of the valuation, a description of the tangible and intangible assets included, and the valuation methodologies employed to arrive at a conclusion of value for the respective assets.

Exhibits comprising:

> *Historical balance sheets and income statements, projections of income, and other valuation schedules that may be too voluminous for the narrative section.*

Appendices consisting of:

Additional description sections that can stand alone, such as discount rate development, abstracts on the use of trend factors, survivor curves.

May also include the appraiser's qualifying comments.

Photographs, if appropriate.

An appraisal report may consist of more than a single volume. It is necessary to enumerate the parts to avoid misunderstanding about what constitutes the full appraisal report.

ABC Company incorporated under New Jersey law in 1970. In that year the Company was established to provide medical equipment, on a contract rental basis, for outpatient, in-home use. . . .

A brief description of the history and nature of the business.

Our valuation of the tangible assets included medical equipment, leasehold improvements, office machinery and equipment, and motor vehicles. Intangible assets appraised include computer software, a leasehold interest, assembled staff, a covenant not to compete, customer contracts, and goodwill and other intangibles. Except as specifically noted in this report, our investigation and appraisal does not include other assets and liabilities or reserves that may appear on the Company's balance sheet.

A recitation of the assets included in and excluded from the appraisal.

In accordance with the above, and in conjunction with the accompanying valuation report, exhibits, and appendices, it is our conclusion that as of January 1, 1987, the amount of $26,443,000 reasonably represents the fair market value of the tangible and intangible assets associated with the ABC Company, distributed as follows:

Asset Classification	Fair Market Value (000s)	Remaining Life (years)
Tangible Assets:		
Medical equipment	$ 9,850	ACRS*
Leasehold improvements	3,500	ACRS*
Office furniture & equipment	820	ACRS*
Motor vehicles	150	ACRS*
Total tangible assets	$14,320	
Intangible Assets:		
Computer software	$ 355	5.0
Leasehold interest	1,240	13.0
Assembled staff	533	N/A
Covenant not to compete	295	3.0
Customer contracts	3,700	2.0
Goodwill	6,000	N/A
Total intangible assets	$12,123	
Total Fair Market Value of All Tangible and Intangible Assets	$26,443	

*Accelerated Cost Recovery System.

The conclusions of fair market value noted above and reported in the accompanying valuation report should not be perceived as the amounts that might be realized from a forced disposition of all or portions of the property in an open market for an alternate use. These values assume that the assets valued are a part of a going concern with prospective profits anticipated to be sufficient to support their reported value.

Emphasis that the reported values are FMV in continued use and not some form of liquidation value. This is a recent development within the appraisal profession to clearly state what the values reported on are and what they are not.

We have not investigated the title to, or any liens, encumbrances, or liabilities against, the subject property.

The property is appraised as if owned free and clear of any encumbrance.

[signature of company principal]
Ace Appraisal Company, Inc.

[signature of responsible appraiser]

Joseph A. Doaks
Supervising Appraiser

NARRATIVE REPORT

The appraisal specifications are repeated to make the narrative section complete in case it becomes separated from the Executive Summary.

INTRODUCTION

We have completed a valuation of the tangible and intangible assets associated with the business enterprise known as the ABC Company, whose corporate offices are located in Mount Laurel, New Jersey. The purpose of this valuation is to express our opinion of the fair market value of these assets as of January 1, 1987. Management of the Acme Company has informed us that these conclusions of value will be utilized to serve as a basis, for financial reporting and income tax purposes, for allocating the purchase price of the ABC Company to the assets acquired.

Fair market value, when that term is used in this report, is defined as the amount at which the property would exchange between a willing buyer and seller, neither being compelled to act, each having knowledge of all relevant facts, with equity to both, and with the assumption that the facilities will remain at their present location for the continuation of the current operations.

In formulating our conclusions of value for these assets as part of a going concern, we have reviewed balance sheets, income statements, and other financial statistics which were furnished by the company and which we accepted as properly representing business operations and conditions.

Our investigation included a review and analysis of this information as well as discussions with management concerning the history and nature of the business, its economic status and prospects and a personal inspection of the company's property which also included a review and analysis of pertinent proprietary information.

Expanded description of the business.

BUSINESS HISTORY AND CHARACTER

ABC Company was incorporated under New Jersey law in 1970. The company was established to provide medical equipment on a contract rental basis for out-patient, in-home use in the tri-state area (Delaware, New Jersey, and Pennsylvania). From 1974 to the present, ABC has increased the scope of its business activities with a great deal of emphasis on market penetration.

The medical equipment and related items comprise adjustable beds, trapeze units and stirrups, powered wheelchairs, walkers, cardiovascular monitors and supporting equipment, portable EKG units, oxygen support systems, oxygen tanks, and other related medical equipment to accommodate heart and stroke victims. At the current time, none of these items is in short supply; however, it is anticipated that some difficulty will develop in procuring certain items in the next year or two. It is believed that technical advancements in the cardiovascular monitors and recent changes in Medicare regulations will contribute to these delays.

ABC's management team is composed of five persons, who have accumulated over 50 years of experience in the medical service and equipment industry. The following table presents a listing of key management personnel:

Name	Position	Age	Years with Company
Mr. Jones, Sr.*	President & Chief Executive Officer	52	14
Mr. Evans	Vice President & Director—Marketing	49	10
Mr. Orr**	Vice Pres.—Marketing & Quality Control	54	14
Mr. Jones, Jr.	Vice President— Customer Service	26	4
Mrs. Wilson	Vice President & Chief Physical Therapist	45	9

*Controlling stockholder.
**Minority stockholder.

If this were an appraisal of ABC's capital stock, this section would include a schedule of major stockholdings.

In addition to the above, ABC employs 45 people as follows:

Sales and marketing 10
Administration 4
Repair technicians 10
Physical therapists 10
Clerks 5
Warehouse and delivery staff 6
Total 45

Overall, management believes that employee relations are good and there is no union representation. Further, management claims that there has not been any attempt to unionize the workforce since its inception in 1970.

Plant location and facilities.

The company's main facility is located at 300 Main Street in Mount Laurel, New Jersey. ABC has done business at this location since 1979 when the facility was leased. The current lease expires in 1999. At the current time ABC does not utilize any other facility; its warehousing, shipping, and showroom are located at this facility.

Description of the customer base.

ABC's equipment as of the valuation date is rented to 875 customers located primarily in the tri-state area. Major users of the equipment include heart and stroke victims, many of whom are senior citizens and Medicare recipients. There are other users of the equipment for various other illnesses and convalescent needs, but such individuals account for less of 10% of the total number of customers.

All of ABC's customers enter into a contract with ABC which is of a standard form and structured on a month-to-month basis. ABC, as a practical matter, cannot extend the terms of their contracts because of the regulations imposed by the U.S. Department of Health, since Medicare patients who enter into long-term medical equipment agreements will not be reimbursed for the cost of rental nor can the company who is renting equipment on a long-term basis expect direct payment from Medicare.

Competition.

In serving its customers ABC vies for business with three other firms. These competitors include H&S, Inc. located in Wilmington, Delaware; the Med-Q Corporation located in Philadelphia, Pennsylvania; and the Baker Company located in Lawrenceville, New Jersey.

Business risks to which ABC is subject.

Successful competition is based on a combination of quality of service, reliability of staff, technical ability, delivery, and rental fees. Among these, technical abilities and rental fees are believed to be the most important.

Review of historical financial performance.

This can be in the form of an "overlay," as here, to substantiate the earnings support for the concluded values or a much more detailed review if the purpose is to value the enterprise or capital stock.

FINANCIAL REVIEW

Attached to this report as Exhibits #1 and #2 are the balance sheets and income statements of the ABC Company. Statements for the period 1982 through 1985 have been certified by the accounting firm of King & King. Statements for the year ended 1986 have been prepared by the company but have yet to receive a certification from the accounting firm. These financial statements, along with other documents and data prepared by the company or on its behalf, have been accepted without verification and are believed to reflect ABC's business operations and financial condition.

Significant accounting policies followed by ABC Company are as follows: inventories are valued at the lower of cost or market and accounted for on a last in, first out (LIFO) basis. Depreciation expenses are computed on an accelerated basis and all capital additions purchased subsequent to December 31, 1980, have been depreciated under the Accelerated Cost Recovery System (ACRS). The company's depreciation policy for financial reporting and income tax purposes are the same.

At December 31, 1986, the company reported total assets of $13.2 million and total stockholders equity of $7.6 million. These accounts have grown on a compounded annual basis of 8.9% and 22% respectively from their 1982 balances. The growth in assets is attributable in part to a 20.5% increase in current assets during the period studied with the most significant increases occurring in cash and short-term investments and accounts receivable. Capital additions have totaled $3.9 million during the period studied with the greatest increase occurring during the period 1986–1985 at which time capital additions totaled $1.5 million. Approximately 85% of these additions were for medical equipment and related items. With respect to shareholders equity, it has been management's policy to avoid or omit dividends. All profits have been retained for the specific purpose of internally funding the expansion of the company's business.

The company's short-term financial picture has improved considerably since 1982. In 1982 the company's current and quick ratio was reported at 0.9 to 1 and 0.8 to 1, respectively, while working capital amounted to a negative $335,000. By 1986 the company's current and quick ratios amounted to 3.5 to 1 and 2.7 to 1, respectively. In the same year working capital amounted to $3.8 million. This improvement is due in part to a substantial increase in the company's receivables and cash and a concerted effort on management's part to reduce accruals and other current liabilities.

Long-term debt consists of a bank loan from a regional bank secured by the company's fixed assets; the loan is priced at 1.5% over the bank's prime lending rate. Because of refinancing in 1986 the loan now has a 5-year term with a balloon payment amounting to $1 million in the fifth year.

Revenues for the 12 months ended December 31, 1986 totalled $16.0 million as compared with $14.0 million reported in the previous year, thus reflecting a 14.3% increase in 1986. Since 1982, total revenues have increased 18.0% on a compounded basis from $8.3 million reported in that year. The company has experienced substantial real growth in direct sales during the period studied. In 1982 direct sales accounted for 5% of total revenues as opposed to 1986 in which direct sales account for 15% of total revenues. It is management's belief that direct sales will not amount to more than 15% of total revenues because of the nature of their business and the markets served. Contract revenues have increased 14.8% on a compounded basis since 1982, growing from $7.8 million to $13.6 million in 1986. Given the nature of the company's business there is a substantial turnover in patient contracts, thus the growth rate reported is more indicative of the inflationary pressures that have affected the medical service industry and, in particular, the medical services industry in the markets served.

During the past five years, net income has increased at an average compound annual rate of 32.6%. The company has experienced growth of net income in almost every year studied; there was an exception, however, in 1984 and 1985, at which time the company experienced a rather flat period. The company's growth in net income is due in part to its ability to control operating expenses and in part to the decline in interest rates. Also, the profit margins on direct sales are substantially higher than that reported for the company as a whole. In 1986 operating margins before depreciation, interest, and taxes amounted to 26.7% for the company, whereas these same margins for direct sales are estimated at 50% by management.

The selected financial statistics reported in the table are intended to provide a financial profile on the ABC Company.

ABC COMPANY FINANCIAL PROFILE

	1986	1985	1984	1983	1982	5 Year Average (1982-1986)[1]
Liquidity:						
Current ratio	3.5:1	2.2:1	1.5:1	1.1:1	0.9:1	1.8:1
Quick ratio	2.7:1	1.7:1	1.2:1	0.9:1	0.8:1	1.5:1
Total liabilities to total assets	0.4:1	0.5:1	0.5:1	0.6:1	0.6:1	0.5:1
Capital Structure:						
Short-term debt (%)	1.6	1.5	1.3	1.3	1.1	1.4
Long-term[2]	36.1	37.6	41.5	44.8	48.9	41.8
Shareholders' equity	62.3	60.9	57.2	53.9	50.0	56.8
Profitability:						
Operating margin before dep., int. & taxes (%)	26.7	23.6	28.0	26.0	26.0	26.1
Return on sales	8.8	7.5	9.0	7.0	6.5	7.8
Return on assets	10.6	8.7	9.4	6.7	5.7	8.2
Return on equity	18.5	17.0	20.4	16.4	15.7	17.6
Growth Rates:						
Total revenues (%)	14.3	20.2	22.6	15.2	–	18.0
Net income	33.3	0.5	56.0	25.0	–	32.6
Total assets	9.3	8.7	10.8	6.8	–	8.9
Working capital	44.6	95.9	236.3	N/A	–	N/A
Shareholders' equity	22.6	20.4	25.6	19.6	–	22.0

[1]Except for growth rates, which are compound growth rates for the period 1982–1986.
[2]Includes current maturities of long-term debt.

In general, the company's liquidity and capital structure position has improved significantly since 1982. This improvement stems from the tremendous improvement in the company's working capital position and cash flow, its profit retention policy, and decline in interest rates during the period studied. Profitability and growth rates have remained relatively consistent with some minor variations occurring in net income during the period 1985–1986.

Description of economic conditions existing as of the appraisal date as well as those existing within the industry segment of the subject company.

INDUSTRY OUTLOOK

As a percentage of the gross national product (GNP), health care expenditures have increased from 6.2% in 1965 to 9.7% in 1986. By 1990 this share could reach or exceed 10.5%, and by 1995 it is expected to reach or exceed 11.5%. This growth has been spurred by an inflation rate in the industry which has been in the double-digit area most years since the 1970s. In 1977 total national health care expenditures amounted to $116.4 billion and by 1986 total expenditures amounted to $356.5 billion, reflecting a compounded growth rate of 13.2%. For the period 1982 through 1986, expenditures grew a compounded rate of 13.5%. After excluding construction and research expenditures for the periods 1982–86 and 1977–86, the growth rate still remains at 13.5%.

The U.S. Congress, perceiving that costs were escalating rapidly, enacted new legislation through the Tax Equity and Fiscal Responsibility Act (TEFRA) which essentially established limits on reimbursements for hospitals' total in-patient operating costs. The new regulations, which took effect October 1, 1983, were to be phased in over the following four years. Under the new rules, health-care providers will not be paid for patient costs above the fixed rates. They will, however, be able to keep any resulting profits, if and when their costs are lower. Furthermore, hospitals will no longer be reimbursed for all of their expenses when they treat Medicare patients. Inefficient practitioners within the health-care and medical services industry will be penalized and low-cost providers will be rewarded. Medicare represents approximately half of all of the revenues in the health-care and medical services industry, therefore almost all hospitals, both publicly and privately owned, will be affected by the new rules.

All of these changes bode well for the ABC Company and its competitors. Since the emphasis in the health-care and medical services industry has switched from total disregard for cost of service to an industry that will have to address itself to cost containment, it is expected that out-of-hospital care will increase. In effect, patients, especially medicare patients, can now expect a longer period of convalescence in their home and a reduced stay in the hospital. Many Medicare patients are treated for various cardiovascular and stroke illnesses and such patients are major users of the type of equipment that ABC rents for in-home patient use. As a result of these new regulations, company management is now anticipating that a greater number of patients will be available at an earlier date and that the in-home convalescence period will be longer than what ABC has traditionally experienced. Also, because of patient uncertainties, the need and demand for other types of equipment will increase. Management is contemplating the addition of other types of equipment to its product line to accommodate those patients who may require a more informative monitoring system due to the existing stage of their illness.

The following table reports the health-care expenditures in the United States for the period 1976 through 1986. Management has concluded that the medical services industry and their company will continue to be affected by high growth and it is their belief that overall growth will range between 7 and 9% over the next three to five years.

Health-Care Industry
Indicated Annual Rates of Growth

Year	Total National Health Expenditures ($ billions)	Annual Rate of Change (%)	Total National Health Expenditures Health Services and Supplies ($ billions)	Annual Rate of Change (%)
1976	103.2	—	96.3	—
1977	116.4	12.8	108.9	13.1
1978	132.7	14.0	124.3	14.1
1979	149.7	12.8	140.6	13.1
1980	169.2	13.0	160.1	13.9
1981	189.3	11.9	179.5	12.1
1982	215.0	13.6	204.5	13.9
1983	249.0	15.8	237.1	15.9
1984	286.6	15.1	273.5	15.4
1985	322.4	12.5	308.2	12.7
1986a	356.5	10.6	339.6	10.2
Compound Growth Rate				
1976–1986		13.2		13.5
1982–1986		13.5		13.5

aIndicates estimated data for 1986.

Source: U.S. Health Care Financing Administration.

BUSINESS ENTERPRISE VALUE

The primary purpose of this valuation analysis is to express a conclusion regarding the fair market value of ABC Company's tangible and intangible assets. However, it is considered essential to the analysis to form a conclusion regarding the value of the total business enterprise. The value of individual assets may then be expressed on the basis of their total contribution to the entire enterprise. The value expressed becomes an opinion of their fair market value, assuming continued use as part of a going concern. The term "business enterprise" is defined as the sum of all tangible and intangible assets plus a normal level of working capital at or near the appraisal date. The total fair market value of these assets also equates to the fair market value of total invested capital, which is defined as the combination of total stockholders' equity and long-term debt.

The valuation of a business enterprise should take into consideration certain factors which may individually or collectively influence the conclusion. Some of these factors may have received specific comment in preceding sections of this report; but in the final analysis, the conclusion of value is primarily dependent upon the adequacy of prospective earnings. The following factors, although not all inclusive, are fundamental and require consideration in determining the fair market value of a business enterprise:

the nature of the business and the history of the enterprise from its inception.

the economic outlook in general and the condition and outlook of the specific industry in particular.

the book value of the enterprise and the financial condition of the business.

the earning capacity of a company.

the dividend paying capacity.

whether or not the enterprise has goodwill or other intangible value.

the market price of stocks of corporations engaged in the same or similar lines of business having their stocks actively traded in a free and open market, either on an exchange or over the counter.

money and capital cost rates, as viewed from a historical, current, and forecasted standpoint and their current and potential effects on the economy, industry, and company.

the company's capital structure and management's operating philosophy relative to the prevailing situation in its industry.

For purposes of this valuation, it was concluded that the most appropriate approach to determine the value of the ABC Company's common stock is the discounted cash flow approach. This conclusion was arrived at only after it was determined that a comparative company analysis would not be appropriate because of the lack of suitable comparative companies.

Projected statements of income and cash flow had been prepared by ABC management. These projections were reviewed in conjunction with the company's historical operations; the near-term prospects for the company and the industry in general; and the reasonableness of the underlying assumptions which drive the forecast. After taking these factors into account, our review of these projections has permitted us to conclude such forecasts are reasonable and may appropriately be used to determine the value of the company based on the discounted cash flow approach. See the accompanying table which reflects the forecast of the ABC Company for the period 1987 through 1992 inclusively.

These cash flows were then discounted at a rate that was deemed appropriate to reflect their present worth. The support for the discount rate may be found in an ap-

ABC Company
Forecast of Income and Net Cash Flow*

	1987	1988	1989	1990	1991	1992
			(in thousands of dollars)			
Sales	2,735	3,145	3,615	4,100	4,585	5,040
Rental Revenue	15,490	17,815	20,485	23,230	25,970	28,560
Total Revenue	18,225	20,960	24,100	27,330	30,555	33,600
Total Operating Expenses	13.670	15,720	17,835	19,950	22,305	24,865
Operating Income, Before Depreciation, Interest and Taxes	4,555	5,240	6,265	7,780	8,250	8,735
Depreciation	1,087	1,262	1,443	1,639	1,848	1,917
Operating Income	3,468	3,978	4,822	6,141	6,402	6,818
Interest Charges, Net of Interest Income	501	432	317	195	103	(18)
Income Before Taxes	2,967	3,546	4,505	5,946	6,299	6,836
Provisions for Income Tax	1,510	1,808	2,303	3,046	3,228	3,505
Net Income	1,457	1,738	2,202	2,900	3,071	3,331
Plus: Depreciation	1,087	1,262	1,443	1,639	1,848	1,917
Gross Cash Flow	2,544	3,000	3,645	4,539	4,919	5,248
Less:						
Capital Expenditures	750	815	875	950	1,010	1,100
Changes in Working Capital	746	684	110	390	371	609
Reductions to Long-term Debt	750	750	750	750	1,025	-
Net Cash Flow	298	751	1,910	2,449	2,513	3,539

*This forecast does not reflect a step-up in value of the tangible and intangible assets, inventories, reserves, or the recapture of depreciation and investment tax credit.

pendix attached to this report. From our analysis reported in the appendix, it was concluded that a discount rate of 14.3% was appropriate for valuation purposes.

As the computations below report, the present worth of ABC's cash flows amount to $21.7 million. However, this aggregate value is based on a discount rate which is reflective of market ratios which are themselves the result of transactions relating to minority shareholdings. Therefore, a premium may be justified by the acquiring company's ability to control the operating characteristics and cash flow of the acquired company. To determine the size of a premium for ABC Company, we reviewed the Analyses & Company's most recent *Merger Review* and concluded, from reported evidence, that a 20% premium would be justified. The computations reported below, based on the aforesaid information, permitted us to conclude that the value for ABC's equity is $26 million.

As previously stated, the business enterprise is determined on the basis of the fair market value of total invested capital which for ABC includes the fair market value of its shareholders' equity at $26 million and reported long-term debt at December 31,

ABC Company
Determination of Business Enterprise Value

Year	Net Cash Flow ($ 000s)	Discount Rate @ 14.3%	Present Worth ($ 000s)	Total ($ 000s)
1987	298	.931	277	
1988	751	.808	607	
1989	1,910	.701	1,339	
1990	2,449	.608	1,489	
1991	2,513	.527	1,324	
1992 (Normal Year)	3,539	.458	1,621	
Capitalized/Terminal Year	35,390*	.426	15,082	
				21,739
Premium @ 20%				4,348
Total				26,087
		Rounded		26,000
		Conclusion		26,000

*Determined by capitalizing the normalized year's net cash flow of $3,539 into perpetuity at a rate of 10%, which itself was arrived at by netting out of the 14% discount rate the expected inflation rate of 4%. Thus the computation is as follows $3,539/0.10 = $35,390. Discount rate is for ½ year in 1987, 1½ years in 1988, etc.

1986, of $4.4 million. Thus the fair market value of the business enterprise for ABC is reasonably concluded to be $30.4 million.

VALUATION OF TANGIBLE ASSETS

There are three generally accepted methods of determining property value: the cost, market, and income approaches.

The cost approach gives consideration to the cost to reproduce or replace the property appraised. From this amount an allowance is deducted to reflect all forms of depreciation. Depreciation may take its form from physical, functional, or economic causes.

The market approach requires an investigation of current prices for similar property. Adjustments may be necessary to reflect the condition and utility of the appraised property relative to its market comparative.

The income approach gives consideration to the present value of the future economic benefits of owning the subject property. This involves the capitalization of a forecasted income stream with due consideration being given to the duration of the income stream and the corresponding risk of achieving it.

With respect to the ABC company, the cost approach was utilized in determining the fair market value of its tangible property. This methodology is appropriate because the equipment is relatively new, is not of special design, purpose, or use, and because the quality of the ABC property record lent itself to the use of this methodology. The cost approach, and in ABC's case the cost of reproduction new, was determined by the trended original cost method which translates the original cost of the item to current cost levels by application of appropriate index numbers.

To employ the trended original cost method, two components are needed. The first being the original cost of the property by vintage year. The second is the appropriate account index numbers which translate the original cost to current cost levels. The result is a statement of value for the specific property item at today's cost levels but with due consideration of the effects of any improvements in techniques and technology.

As a result of ABC's property record being separated into accounts by vintage year, the application of trends by account classifications was chosen for development of the reproduction cost new. Typical office furniture and equipment accounts consisted of desks, chairs, credenzas, calculators, typewriters, computers, and peripheral equipment; leasehold improvement accounts consisted of floor and wall coverings, drop ceilings, and specialized lighting. The medical equipment accounts included adjustable beds, trapeze apparatus, various cardiovascular equipment and monitors, walkers, and powered wheelchairs, to name just a few. Indexes for these accounts were obtained from publications of the United States government and the U.S. Health Care Finance Administration. To determine the reasonableness of these trends to the cost in the property record, a verification based on random sample was made of current unit prices. The result was that there is a very high correlation between current prices and the reproduction costs using the indexing method.

In general, depreciation for valuation purposes must reflect the loss of value or service utility. With respect to physical depreciation, an average economic service life was assigned to each property item. These lives were discussed with ABC personnel and were judged to be reasonable. This age-life technique to quantify physical depreciation was developed for each vintage group. This depreciation reflects the loss in value of the property due to wear and tear.

A minor degree of functional obsolescence was identified in certain cardiovascular monitoring items. No other functional obsolescence could be identified in the property items appraised.

The cost approach must also take into account any additional deduction for economic obsolescence. As previously reported, it is concluded that the prospective earnings of the company are sufficient to justify an investment in the tangible assets at the concluded costs of reproduction new less depreciation. Therefore, no economic obsolescence will effect the ABC property.

A portion of the tangible assets appraised were valued at original cost. These assets include any capital additions within the six-month period of July 1, 1986, to December 31, 1986.

As a result of the considerations and calculations noted above, we have concluded that the fair market value for the tangible assets is as follows:

Asset Classification	Fair Market Value ($000s)
Medical Equipment	9,850
Leasehold Improvements	3,500
Office Furniture & Equipment	820
Motor Vehicles	150
Total	14,320

The above-stated values are indicative of fair market value on a going concern basis and, as such, these values should not be perceived as the amount that might be realized from a forced disposition of all or portions of the property.

VALUATION OF INTANGIBLE ASSETS

The valuation of intangible assets requires that all relevant factors be taken into consideration to determine value. Like tangible property, value for intangible assets may be determined by any one or a combination of the cost, market, or income approaches. The income approach provides an indication of value based on the present worth of the future economic benefits attributable to the intangible asset. The cost approach involves an estimate of the cost to replace the specific asset, less an amount representing obsolescence, where applicable. The market approach involves a survey and investigation of current market prices for the same or similar type asset.

A detailed description and the valuation of the intangible assets associated with the company follow.

Computer Software

The valuation of computer software has been determined on the basis of its estimated cost to replace, giving due consideration to all forms of depreciation which, in the case of computer software, consists essentially of any functional obsolescence that may be present in the existing programs. Nearly all the software systems were judged to be unique to company operations in such a degree that there are no reasonably comparable software packages on the market for purchase.

Discussions were held with the company's data-processing manager concerning each software system. Consideration was given to current levels of wages, salaries, fringe benefits, overhead, and computer expenses that would be incurred in the replacement of the present computer software system.

Based on the analysis detailed in the table which follows this section, it is estimated that reproducing the existing software system would cost approximately $426,000 at current labor and overhead costs.

A factor for functional obsolescence is deducted to reflect the loss in utility because of changing requirements. That is, the requirements of the users of computerized information are continually changing. Therefore a computer program, unless it
is very new, nearly always falls short of satisfying the current user needs. The amount
of this short-fall is reflected as a loss of utility. Computer systems can also suffer functional obsolescence because of inefficient running time, little-used programming lan-
guages, or dependence upon obsolete hardware. As a result of our consideration of
these factors, the replacement cost less depreciation is calculated to be $354,583,
and fair market value was concluded to be $355,000 for the ABC Company's com-
puter software system. Given the level of changes and modification that management has incorporated into its existing system over the years, a remaining life of five
years is considered appropriate for this asset. Our investigation failed to establish any
reason to assume a shorter life for this asset than is currently advocated.

Leasehold Interest

A leasehold interest exists for the lessee when the fixed contract rate in the lease is
less than the current market rent for comparable property. The valuation requires an
analysis of:

existing lease.
investigation of current market rentals.
capitalization of net cash flow benefits over the remaining term of the lease.

Our analysis of ABC's lease contract is reported in the following abstract.

ABC Company
Abstract of Lease Contract

Landlord:	JFB & Associates
Tenant:	ABC Company
Contract Date:	December 15, 1978
Effective:	January 1, 1979
Leased Premise:	300 Main Street, Mount Laurel, NJ 08051 —a two-story, 100,000-square-foot facility which includes 50,000 square feet for office use and 50,000 square feet of unimproved space for commercial & office use.
Use of Facility:	Office & Commercial
Term:	20 years, effective January 1, 1979
Expiration Date:	December 31, 1999
Contract Rent:	$10.25 per square foot under current option
Taxes & Operating Expenses:	Tenant responsibility
Repairs:	Landlord responsibilities include and are limited to: all structural and exterior repairs, heating, plumbing, air conditioning, electric lines (from installation)

ABC Company

Fair Market Value of Computer Software

System Descr.	Number of Programs	Total Lines of Code	Current Usable Lines of Code	Man-years Required to Replace Existing System	Fully Burdened Daily Labor Rate ($)	Replacement Cost Before Obsolescence ($)	Allowance for Obsolescence (%)	Replacement Cost Less Depreciation ($)	Indicated Fair Market Value ($)
Patient Listing & Demographics	20	1,950	1,950	0.50	139.84	18,179	-	18,179	18,180
Accts. Receivable	30	2,925	2,340	0.75		27,269	20	21,815	21,815
Accounts Payable	9	880	705	0.25		9,090	20	7,272	7,275
Purchasing	21	2,045	1,535	0.50		18,179	25	13,634	13,635
Inventory Control	40	3,900	2,925	1.00		36,358	25	27,269	27,270
Service Report	45	4,390	2,855	1.13		41,084	35	26,705	26,705
Payroll	31	3,020	2,565	0.75		27,269	15	23,179	23,180
Personnel	28	2,730	2,185	0.75		27,269	20	22,815	22,815
Scheduling	46	4,485	3,140	1.00		36,358	30	25,450	25,450
Budget	23	2,240	1,790	0.50		18,179	20	14,543	14,545
Incentive Report	35	3,410	2,045	0.88		31,995	40	19,197	19,200
General Ledger	44	4,290	4,290	1.10		39,994	-	39,994	39,994
Standard Costs— Update	14	1,365	1,365	0.35		12,725	-	12,725	12,725
Property Control	90	8,775	8,775	2.25		81,806	-	81,806	81,810
Total	476	46,405	38,465			425,754		354,583	354,600

We investigated current market rents for the same or similar types of facility as currently occupied by ABC Company. The result of the market investigation is reported in the following table. Note that most of the comparable properties are of similar size and close proximity to the ABC Company and, further, current market rents range from a low of $11.50 per square foot to a high of $14.75 per square foot.

ABC Company
Leasehold Interest Comparative Analysis

	Comparative				
	#1	#2	#3	#4	#5
Location	350 East Marlton Pk. Cherry Hill, NJ	21 Main St. Moorestown, NJ	4545 Rt 130 North Cinnaminson, NJ	600 West Rt 38 Cherry Hill, NJ	2140 South Rt 73 Maple Shade, NJ
Available Space (sq. ft)	90,000	110,000	75,000	85,000	130,000
Principal Contact	Landlord	Landlord	Agent	Landlord	Agent
Lease Terms & Conditions	Standard	Standard	Standard	Standard	Options to renew in 5-yr. intervals up to maximum of 3 renewals from base period
Rental Rate (Sq. Ft.)	$14.75	$12.00	$11.50	$14.00	$13.85 base period only
Occupied	recently	to take possession in 30 days	available for approx. 6 weeks	recently	recently occupied 50% of capacity

From this investigation, giving due consideration to adjustments for space, location, physical features, time, and other factors, it is concluded that the current market rent for the subject leased space is fairly stated in the amount of $13.00 per square foot.

The lessee's rental advantage is the difference between the current market rent of $13.00 per square foot and the contract rent of $10.25 per square foot. Thus an annual rental advantage of $2.75 per square foot exists which in the aggregate amounts to $275,000. This $275,000 savings as of the appraisal date will exist for the remaining term of the lease contract. The present worth of these future rental savings has been determined using a discount rate of 20%. The computations which support the conclusion of value for the leasehold interest are as follows:

$$\$275,000 \times 4.533 = \$1,246,487 \text{ (rounded to } \$1,240,000)$$

From the above computations, it is concluded that the fair market value of the lease-hold interest is $1,240,000 with a remaining life of 13 years.

Assembled Staff

The valuation of this asset gives recognition to the benefits associated with having an assembled labor and management staff. An investor acquiring all of the assets of the business enterprise, but not the existing staff, would have to incur the costs associated with their replacement. Therefore, value should be viewed in terms of the cost savings that Acme will enjoy derived from the benefit of having an assembled staff ready and available.

Cost involved in replacing an assembled staff may be a one-time cost or variable cost, depending upon the organizational position and requirement for training.

For the company, an indication of value was calculated premised on a cost-to-replace basis. Certain costs incurred in the normal course of recruiting and training a workforce by employee classification can be isolated and quantified. As noted in the table which follows, recruitment costs may be defined to include advertising costs, agency fees, relocation expenses, interviewing expenses, and other miscellaneous employment costs.

Training costs are defined to include the non-productive time that an employee in training spends to acquire on-the-job proficiency and knowledge of peripheral job routines, company locations, customers and practices and work flows.

It should be noted that these costs do not include any elements of value, such as accumulated know-how, that do not decrease in value over time; only costs that must be incurred by the company when an employee terminates are considered.

From the table, fair market value for the assembled staff is reasonably concluded to be $533,000. Attempts to quantify a remaining life for the workforce proved unsuccessful because of lack of sufficient data, though it is certainly reasonable to expect that, over a period of time, the present workforce will be eliminated by normal attrition.

Covenant Not to Compete

Included in the assets acquired is a covenant not to compete between Messrs. Jones and Orr and the company. This covenant is effective for a three-year period ending December 31, 1989. The covenant prohibits Messrs. Jones and Orr from competing against Acme anywhere in the United States. Acme for its part has guaranteed Messrs. Jones and Orr employment and income through the issuance of a personal service contract. Messrs. Jones and Orr have considerable knowledge, expertise, and contacts within the business. Their leaving the ABC Company would cause a definite loss to ABC and Acme, and both men would represent a formidable competitive challenge either currently or in the future should they decide to compete against ABC and Acme.

The covenant was valued on the basis of the estimated effect on the profits of the

ABC Company
Fair Market Value of Assembled Staff

Employee Classification	Population Size	Salary Mid-point ($)	Benefits and Overhead (%)	Fully Burdened Labor Costs ($)	Non-Productive Training and Disruption Period (months)	Costs ($)	Recruitment Rate (%)	Recruitment Costs ($)	Aggregate Replacement Costs[2] ($)	Fair Market Value ($)
Officers	5	125,000	35	168,750	1.0	14,006	35	41,250	276,280	276,280
Administration	4	25,000	20	30,000	0.5	1,260	25	6,250	30,040	30,040
Sales & Marketing	10	30,000	20	36,000	0.75	2,232	25	7,500	97,320	97,320
Technicians	10	20,000	20	24,000	1.0	1,992	20	4,000	59,920	59,920
Physical Therapists	10	20,000	20	24,000	1.0	1,992	20	4,000	59,920	59,920
Clerks	5	14,000	20	16,800	0.5	706	-	100[1]	4,030	4,030
Warehouse & Delivery	6	15,000	20	18,000	0.5	756	-	100[1]	5,136	5,140
	50								532,646	532,650

[1]Recruitment costs for this class of employee are estimated at $100 per employee.

[2]Determined by multiplying the sum of columns 6 and 8 with column 1.

Case	Period (Year Ended)	Probability of Remaining (%)	Probability as a Competitive Factor (%)	Actual Probability
1	1987	80	20	.20
2	1988	65	35 (.8 × .35)	.28
3	1989	50	50 (.8 × .35 × .5)	.14

company if both employees were to leave the company during the period of the agreement multiplied by the probability of their leaving if there were no covenant. The value of the covenant to Acme comes from its recognition of economic realities. That is, if both men were not constrained by the covenant, they would be free to exercise their expertise and knowledge of the business and industry either for an ABC competitor or for themselves.

It is reasoned that if either man left on his own, he would have a minimal effect on the company's earnings; therefore, we have considered the effect of both men leaving together. It was further reasoned that only the contract revenue would be affected since they would have the greatest effect on this stream of income.

It is estimated that the probability of leaving for both men would increase in each successive year of the three-year period as reported in the probability table above.

Determination of the value for the covenant not to compete is presented in the following table. This table contains a projected income statement for the base case, which assumes both executives remain with the company. It also includes the projected earnings assuming both men were to leave in each of the three years covered by the covenant. The difference, or loss in earnings, is then multiplied by the cumulative probability of their leaving in each year. The respective amounts are then present valued using a 22% discount rate.

From the foregoing analysis the present value of future earnings losses amounts to $241,000.

In addition to the net income losses the company would suffer should both men leave, the company would also incur the added expense of recruiting and training replacement executives. This additional cost was estimated using a combined base annual salary of $250,000. Initial costs were adjusted to reflect a 5% annual rate of inflation. The present value of these costs was determined based upon a 22% discount rate. The costs are then multiplied by the probability factors for each year as previously discussed.

ABC Company
Covenant Not to Compete

	1987	1988	1989	Total
		(in thousands of dollars)		
Base Case:				
Contract Revenues	15,490	17,815	20,485	
After-tax Profit Margin on Contract Revenues				
	867	1,033	1,332	
Extent of Net Income Lost Due to Absence of Jones and Orr	50%	30%	10%	
	$ 433	$ 310	$ 133	
Reflecting Case 1:				
Probability Factor	.20	.20	.20	
Probable Income Loss	$87	$62	$27	
Discount Rate @ 22%	.906	.743	.609	
Net Present Value	$79	$46	$16	$141
Reflecting Case 2:				
Probability Factor	-	.28	.28	
Probable Income Loss	-	$87	$37	
Discount Rate @ 22%	-	.743	.609	
Net Present Value	-	$65	$23	88
Reflecting Case 3:				
Probability Factor	-	-	.14	
Probable Income Loss	-	-	$19	
Discount Rate @ 22%	-	-	.609	
Net Present Value	-	-	$12	12
Total				$241

Cost incurred to replace Mr. Jones and Mr. Orr:

Recruitment	Market Salaries:	President	$150,000	
		Vice President	100,000	
	Combined Total		$250,000	
	Recruitment Fees		33%	
	Recruitment Costs			$ 82,500
Disruption	Amounting to 1 month fully burdened labor cost. Thus, officer labor burden amounts to 30% of base			26,975
Total Replacement Costs				$109,475

From previously determined probability factors and an annual rate of inflation of 5%, the present worth of these replacement costs are determined.

Year	Replacement Costs	×	Inflation Factor	×	Discount Rate @ 22%	×	Actual Probability Factor	=	Present Worth
1	$109,475		-		.906		.20		$19,837
2	109,475		1.05		.703		.28		23,914
3	109,475		1.103		.609		.14		10,295
	Total								54,046
							Rounded		54,000

The fair market value of the covenant not to compete, which has a remaining life of three years, is concluded to be $295,000, determined as follows:

Present value of lost revenue	$241,000
Present value of future replacement costs	54,000
Total	$295,000

Customer Contracts

As of the valuation date, ABC Company had customer contracts totaling 875, a majority of which were for cardiovascular and stroke-related equipment. The balance of the company's contracts were for equipment rented to patients with some form of physical handicap.

All of the contracts are of a standard form and structured on a month-to-month basis. ABC, as a practical matter, cannot extend the terms of its contracts because of regulations imposed by the U.S. Department of Health for Medicare patients. Medicare patients who enter into long-term medical equipment agreements will not be reimbursed for the cost of rental nor can the company renting the equipment on a long-term basis expect direct payment from Medicare.

Approximately 90% of ABC's patients are Medicare recipients. As previously indicated, the types of equipment rented by ABC to this group are intended for the seriously ill heart patient and the stroke-afflicted individual, which are illnesses that generally affect the senior citizen population, many of whom are dependent upon Medicare. Therefore, it is good business practice on ABC's part to adhere to Medicare regulations, since a significant portion of ABC's business comes from this market segment.

The value of the customer contracts has been determined by the income approach. However, for the valuation of the customer contracts to be complete, the average total life of all customer contracts that existed as of the valuation date, as well as the average remaining life of all customer contracts on the same date, needed to be computed.

Exhibit 3 of this report is the result of a detailed analysis of the historical activity of the customer contracts. Analysis of customer contract turnover data for the period December 31, 1984, to December 31, 1986 produces the survivor curve shown at the bottom of Exhibit 3. The numerical equivalent is shown in Column 2 at the top of that page. The remaining columns in that table illustrate the calculation of the area under the survivor curve to the right of various year points, which area is representative of remaining service life for various contract ages.

The valuation of the customer contracts proceeds from this analysis, recognizing that the income stream attributable to the contracts will decline in the future according to the same pattern exhibited in the past. This assumes, of course, that future conditions will be similar to those in the past, a reasonable assumption in this particular case.

Customer contract revenues as of the valuation date approximated $13.6 million. Tabulation of these revenue dollars for the customer contracts outstanding and the associated survival study provide an indication of fair market value.

Line 1 of the table forecasts those customer contracts surviving over their remaining life. Line 2 reports customer contract revenues for the 12 months ended December 31, 1987, which amounts to approximately $14.4 million. For valuation purposes, these revenues were adjusted for an average long-term rate of growth of 6%. Line 3 is the result of multiplying line 1 by line 2. Line 4 reflects the operating margins that will result from the servicing of these contracts. It is important to note that these operating margins reflect only those costs that will be incurred to service existing contracts. Lines 5 and 6 are, in general, explanatory; however, it is important to note that these depreciation and amortization charges as well as returns on assets employed were computed on the basis of the fair market value of those assets. The purpose of reflecting a return on assets employed is to isolate the income stream that is immediately attributable to the customer contracts, which is reported on line 8.

Since these income streams are declining over a 10-year period from valuation date, it was necessary to reflect the present worth of these future income streams. Line 9 reports discount rates over the 10-year period at 20% and line 10 reports the present worth of this income stream as determined by multiplying line 9 by line 8. From the foregoing analysis and the data reported in the attached schedules, the fair market value of the customer contracts is $3.7 million with an average remaining life of two years.

Goodwill

In addition to the tangible and specifically identified intangible assets discussed above, another intangible asset associated with the business is goodwill. In this report we refer to goodwill as including the elements of a going concern in addition to the traditional element of patronage.

Goodwill has been valued by a residual approach whereby the values of other identified assets are subtracted from the value of the business enterprise as a whole to indicate an amount attributable to this asset.

ABC Company
Valuation of Customer Contracts

Line #	Year Number	1987 1	1988 2	1989 3	1990 4	1991 5	1992 6	1993 7	1994 8	1995 9	1996 10
1	Percent Surviving at Mid-Year Based on Maximum Life of 10 Years	.85	.55	.31	.17	.11	.08	.05	.03	.015	.01
2	Customer Contract Revenue (@ Dec. 31, 1986 of $13,600; Adjusted to Reflect Average Long-term Annual Rate of growth of 6%	$14,416	$15,289	$16,198	$17,170	$18,200	$19,292	$20,449	$21,676	$22,997	$24,356
3	Customer Contract Revenue Based on Survival Estimates	12,254	8,405	5,021	2,919	2,002	1,543	1,022	650	345	244
4	Operating Margin (which reflects only those costs necessary to maintain contracts)	60% 7,352	60% 5,043	60% 3,013	60% 1,751	60% 1,201	60% 926	60% 613	60% 390	60% 207	60% 146
5	Less: Depreciation and Amortization Charges	2,094	1,355	764	394	255	37	23	14	5	4
6	Less: Pre-tax Return on Assets Employed	2,115	1,167	543	243	122	83	48	27	12	8
7	Pre-tax Contract Income	3,143	2,521	1,706	1,114	824	806	542	349	190	134
8	Net Income Attributable to Customer Contracts	$ 1,572	$ 1,260	$ 853	$ 557	$ 412	$ 403	$ 271	$ 175	$ 95	$ 67
9	Discount Rate (@ 20%	.914	.762	.635	.529	.441	.367	.306	.255	.213	.177
10	Present Worth	$ 1,437	$ 960	$ 542	$ 295	$ 182	$ 148	$ 83	$ 45	$ 20	$ 12

Total $3,724 (Rounded to $3,700)

The residual approach requires that provision be made for an amount of working capital at the appraisal date. From the most recent balance sheet data, we conclude that net working capital in the amount of $3.8 million is an appropriate provision.

Under the residual method, the following calculation indicates the value of goodwill and other intangibles:

ABC Company
Valuation of Goodwill—Residual Method

		($ 000s)
Fair Market Value of		
Total Shareholders' Equity	26,000	
Long-Term Debt	4,400	
Total Value of Invested Capital/		
Business Enterprise Value		30,400
Less: Provisions for Working Capital		3,810
Amount Allocable to Tangible and		
Intangible Assets		$26,590
Less Fair Market Value of		
Tangible Assets:		
Medical equipment	9,850	
Leasehold improvements	3,500	
Office furniture & equipment	820	
Motor vehicles	150	
Total tangible assets	$14,320	
Amount Allocable to Intangible Assets		12,270
Less: Fair Market Value of		
Intangible Assets:		
Computer software	355	
Leasehold interest	1,240	
Assembled staff	533	
Covenant not to compete	295	
Customer contracts	3,700	
Total identifiable intangible assets	$ 6,123	
Indicated Value of Goodwill		$ 6,147

On the basis of this computation, we conclude a value for goodwill and other unidentified intangibles in the amount of $6 million.

CONCLUSION OF VALUES

Based upon the investigation and analysis as set forth in this report, it is concluded that the fair market value of the tangible and intangible assets of the ABC Company as of January 1, 1987, is $26,443,000, distributed as follows:

ABC Company
Tangible and Intangible Assets—Fair Market Value

Asset Classification	Fair Market Value ($ 000s)	Remaining Life (years)
Tangible Assets:		
Medical equipment	9,850	ACRS*
Leasehold improvements	3,500	ACRS*
Office furniture & equipment	820	ACRS*
Motor vehicles	150	ACRS*
Total tangible assets	14,320	
Intangible Assets:		
Computer software	355	5.0
Leasehold interest	1,240	13.0
Assembled staff	533	N/A
Covenant not to compete	295	3.0
Customer contracts	3,700	2.0
Goodwill	6,000	N/A
Total intangible assets	12,123	
Total Fair Market Value of All Tangible and Intangible Assets	26,443	

*Accelerated Cost Recovery System

EXHIBIT 1

ABC Company
Comparative Historical Balance Sheet Data

	1986	1985	1984	1983	1982	Compound Growth Rate 1982–1986
			(in thousands of dollars)			
Current Assets						
Cash and short term investments	$ 650	$ 400	$ 450	$ 475	$ 355	
Accounts receivable, Net	3,500	5,235	2,550	2,095	1,815	
Inventory	800	620	500	215	325	
Other current assets	400	575	300	85	45	
Total current assets	5,350	4,830	3,800	3,070	2,540	20.5%
Gross Fixed Assets	16,100	14,600	13,900	12,900	12,200	7.2
Less: Accumulated depreciation	8,300	7,400	6,635	5,985	5,395	
Net Fixed Assets	7,800	7,200	7,265	6,915	6,805	3.5
Total Assets	$13,150	$12,030	$11,065	$ 9,985	$ 9,345	8.9
Liabilities & Shareholders' Equity:						
Current Liabilities						
Short-term debt	$ 200	$ 150	$ 120	$ 100	$ 75	
Current maturities of long-term debt	375	175	250	175	300	
Accruals and other current liabilities	965	1,870	2,085	2,395	2,500	
Total current liabilities	1,540	2,195	2,455	2,670	2,875	(14.4)
Long-Term Debt (bank note)	4,025	3,650	3,475	3,225	3,050	7.2
Total Liabilities	5,565	5,845	5,930	5,895	5,925	(1.6)
Total Shareholders' Equity	7,585	6,185	5,135	4,090	3,420	22.0%
Total Liabilities & Shareholders' Equity	$13,150	$12,030	$11,065	$ 9,985	$ 9,245	
Working Capital	$ 3,810	$ 2,635	$ 1,345	$ 400	$ (335)	

Source: Data provided by ABC Company.

EXHIBIT 2

ABC Company
Comparative Historical Income Statement Data
(in thousands of dollars)

	1986		1985		1984		1983		1982		Compound Growth Rate 1982–1986
Sales	$ 2,400	15.0%	$ 1,820	13.0%	$ 1,165	10.0%	$ 950	10.0%	$ 415	5.0%	55.1%
Contract Revenues	13,600	85.0	12,180	87.0	10,485	90.0	8,550	90.0	7,835	95.0	14.8
Total Revenues	$16,000	100.0%	$14,000	100.0%	$11,650	100.0%	$9,500	100.0%	$8,250	100.0%	18.0
Operating Expenses: Salaries, wages & fringe benefits	2,060		1,680		1,455		1,235		1,030		18.9
Marketing, advertising & promotion	5,300		4,960		3,810		3,185		2,790		17.4
General & administrative	4,368		4,056		3,123		2,610		2,285		17.6
Total Operating expenses	11,728	73.3	10,696	76.4	8,388	72.0	7,030	74.0	6,105	74.0	17.7
Income Before Depreciation, Interest, & Income Taxes	4,272	26.7	3,304	23.6	3,262	28.0	2,470	26.0	2,145	26.0	18.8
Depreciation	900		765		650		590		550		13.1
Operating Income	3,372	21.0	2,539	18.1	2,612	22.4	1,880	19.8	1,595	19.3	20.6
Interest Charges, Net of Interest Income	630		560		600		615		625		
Income Before Income Taxes	2,742	17.1	1,979	14.1	2,012	17.3	1,265	13.3	970	11.8	29.7
Income Taxes	1,342		929		967		565		434		
Net Income	$ 1,400	8.8%	$ 1,050	7.5%	$ 1,045	9.0%	$ 670	7.0%	$ 536	6.5%	32.6%

Source: Data provided by ABC Company.

EXHIBIT 3

ABC Company
Economic Remaining Life of Customer Contracts

Year (1)	Percent Surviving		Cumulative Area (4)	Remaining Life (5)
	Beg. Yr. (2)	Mid-Yr. (3)		
1	100	.850	2.170	2.170
2	70	.550	1.320	1.886
3	40	.310	.770	1.925
4	21	.170	.460	2.190
5	13	.110	.290	2.231
6	9	.080	.180	2.000
7	6	.050	.100	1.667
8	4	.030	.050	1.250
9	2	.015	.020	1.000
10	1	.005	.005	.500

Column 4 equals the cumulative sum of Column 3 and represents the area under the curve.

Column 5 equals Column 4/Column 2 and represents the expected remaining life at various ages.

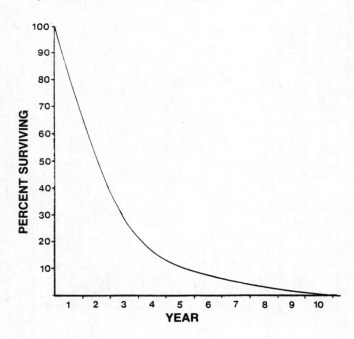

APPENDIX A

DISCOUNT RATE DEVELOPMENT

The value of a business and its assets generally reflects the present worth of the future economic benefits to be derived from ownership. A fundamental consideration therefore is quantification of the risk and return trade-off that is associated with the achievement of future economic benefits; higher risk demands higher return. Throughout our analysis a discount rate has been used in the valuation of specific assets. The discount rate reflects an appropriate rate of return on an investment similar to ABC Company and its assets with respect to business risk, purchasing-power risk, interest-rate risk, economic risk, and industry risk.

In formulating an opinion regarding a proper rate of return for application to ABC and its business assets the starting point is to review the yields on selected securities as listed below:

Security	Yield (%)
90-day certificate of deposit	5.75
6-month treasuries	5.39
Long-term treasuries	7.72
Corporate bonds, Aaa	8.56
Corporate bonds, Baa	9.99
Prime rate	7.50

Source: U.S. Financial Data, December 31, 1986. Federal Rserve Bank of St. Louis.

Ranked from lowest to highest risk it is evident that as the perception of risk increases the rate of return required by investors increases. Treasury securities are considered one of the safest investments because of the credit worthiness and backing of the United States government. These investments are nearly risk-free and have the greatest assurance regarding the amount and timing of the investment returns of principal. Higher yields are provided on corporate bonds for these issues carry greater risk.

Debt securities generally possess superior rights over equity investments and are often secured by property. Equity investment returns must therefore reflect the additional risks over those of secure debtors. Indicators of an appropriate equity rate for valuing ABC Company are derived from an analysis of equity returns provided by investments in companies that are effected to a similar degree by the same types of business, purchasing power, interest rate, and economic and industry risks. Indications of a proper equity rate of return are developed from application of the capital asset pricing model (CAPM). This model attempts to describe the way prices of individual securities are determined in efficient markets. Conceptually, the capital asset pricing model states that the expected rate of return on a security is determined as a risk-free rate plus a risk premium. The amount of risk premium reflects the specific and additional risks associated with the business of ABC and the possible loss of investment. The capital asset pricing model is presented below.

$$Re = Rf + B (Rm - Rf)$$

where:

Re: required rate of return.

Rf: the risk-free rate of return reflecting the rates as demanded by investors where the safety of principal is guaranteed and the anticipated return on investment is assured. Typically this rate is equated to the long-term treasury securities.

B: the measure of volatility of a particular investment return in relation to the stock returns of a broad market portfolio. The susceptibility of returns to macroeconomic forces such as inflation and federal reserve policy are measured by a statistical analysis of the past returns.

Rm: the expected return on a market portfolio.

A risk-free rate of return was selected after reference to the weekly publication of the Federal Reserve Bank of St. Louis, *U.S. Financial Data*. The yield on long-term securities at December 30, 1986, was 7.72 percent. Development of a beta appropriate for application to ABC was developed from analysis of betas calculated by Merrill Lynch in *Security Risk Evaluation*. The betas for each of the publicly traded companies that are considered comparable to ABC were reviewed and an average was used as an indication of the volatility associated with an investment in the company. The following list of comparable companies with accompanying beta factors was derived from *Security Risk Evaluation*.

Company	Beta
Healthy, Inc.	1.01
Con Glomerate Co.	0.46
Supplier Incorporated	1.07
Beds for Everyone	0.57
Medical, Inc.	0.76
Oxy Gen Corp.	1.02
Racing Wheelchairs Co.	1.47
Average	0.92

Based upon the average beta and that of companies most like ABC, a reasonable beta for application to the capital asset pricing model equals 1.0.

A review of Anderson Associates' annual report on expected market returns provided an indication that companies comprising the New York Stock Exchange earned a return of 6% over the risk-free rate (Rm − Rf). The analysis covered trends from 1926 to the present. The report further showed that the return of the market over the risk-free rate for the smallest one-fifth of the stocks traded on the New York Stock Exchange equals 9%. Application of CAPM suggests that an appropriate discount rate for use in our analysis has an equity rate of return equal to 17%.

$$Re = Rf + B (Rm − Rf)$$
$$= 7.72 + 1.0 (9.0)$$
$$= 7.72 + 9.0$$
$$= 16.72\%$$

An appropriate weighted average cost of capital can be developed by assuming a 25% debt to 75% equity capital structure with a 10% debt cost and 17% equity cost. Utilizing a long-term, overall 40% income tax rate translates to an after-tax cost of debt of 6.0% (because of the deductibility of interest expenses). The weighted average cost of capital considered appropriate for application to the entire business enterprise of ABC translates to 14.3%.

Type of Capital	Capital Structure (%)	Cost Rate (%)	After-Tax Cost Rate (%)	Weighted (%)
Debt	25	10.0	6.0	1.50
Equity	75	17.0	17.0	12.25
				14.25

The business enterprise of ABC, like many other companies, is composed of various asset categories which include net working capital, fixed assets, and intangible assets. The appropriate weighted average cost of capital (determined to be 14.3%) reflects an appropriate rate of return from the integrated collection of the asset categories. A proper rate of return for specific assets would be higher or lower depending upon risk elements such as transferability, liquidity, asset versatility regarding strategic redeployment, and other factors. Asset classification rates of return are listed below.

Asset Classification	Required Rate of Return (%)
Net working capital	7.0
Fixed assets	13.0
Intangible assets	20.0
Overall business enterprise	14.3

Net working capital is assigned a lower required rate of return reflecting the liquid nature of the components that comprise working capital. Fixed assets, on the other hand, lack the same degree of liquidity and may represent a more difficult asset to re-deploy toward new strategies. A higher rate of return is usually associated with the fixed assets of an enterprise. Finally, intangible assets such as leasehold interests, covenant not to compete, and customer contracts have the highest degree of risk. Although these assets can be shown to contribute significantly to the profitability of the overall enterprise, they also possess characteristics such as the least likelihood of transferability, the lowest possibility of redeployment should strategic planning changes occur, poor liquidity, and so on. As part of the overall enterprise, intangible assets would represent components with the highest amount of risk.

Based upon this analysis we have used appropriate rates of return throughout this report where specific assets have been valued by an income approach.

SERVICE CONDITIONS

Neither Ace Appraisal Company, its officers, or its professional staff have an interest in any property that is the subject of this valuation report. We use the term "interest" to mean ownership of the property; acting, or having some expectation of acting, as agent in the purchase, sale, or financing of the property; or acting as the manager of the property.

Ace Appraisal Company or its officers have not conditioned their fee for service either as a percentage of the value conclusion or on any other contingency that is related to the outcome of an award, court action, tax reduction, consummation of a sale, financing, or specified finding by the client.

This report is made only for the purpose stated and the written permission of Ace Appraisal Company is required before all or any portions of it are made public.

The information identified in this report as being furnished by others is believed to be reliable, but no responsibility for its accuracy is assumed.

APPENDIX

AMERICAN SOCIETY OF APPRAISERS
Airline Pilots Association Building
535 Herndon Parkway
Herndon, Virginia 22070
(703)478-2228
Mailing address:
Post Office Box 17265
Washington D.C. 20041

AMERICAN INSTITUTE OF REAL
  ESTATE APPRAISERS of the
  NATIONAL ASSOCIATION OF
  REALTORS®
430 North Michigan Avenue
Chicago, Illinois 60611–4088
(312)329-8559

SOCIETY OF REAL ESTATE
  APPRAISERS®
645 North Michigan Avenue
Chicago, Illinois 60611–2881
(312)346-7422

THE CANADIAN INSTITUTE OF
  CHARTERED BUSINESS
  VALUATORS
(Institut canadien des experts en
evaluation d'enterprises)
121 Bloor Street East
3rd Floor
Toronto, Ontario M4W 3M5
(416)960-1254

APPRAISAL INSTITUTE OF CANADA
Institut Canadien des Evaluateurs
93 Lombard Avenue
Suite 309
Winnipeg, Manitoba R3B 3B1
(204)942-0751

BIBLIOGRAPHY

VALUATION, DEPRECIATION, LIFE ANALYSIS

Engineering Valuation and Depreciation, Anson Marston, Robley Winfrey, Jean C. Hempstead, 1953, Iowa State University Press, Ames, Iowa.

Appraisal Principles and Procedures, Henry A. Babcock, FASA, 1980, American Society of Appraisers, Washington, D.C.

Depreciation—Accounting, Taxes, and Business Decisions, Joseph D. Coughlan, William K. Strand, 1969, The Ronald Press Company, New York.

Principles of Engineering Economy, Eugene L. Grant, W. Grant Ireson, Richard S. Leavenworth, 1976, John Wiley & Sons, Inc., New York.

Statistical Analyses of Industrial Property Retirements, Robley Winfrey, revised 1967 by Harold A. Cowles, 1967, Engineering Research Institute, Iowa State University, Ames, Iowa.

Public Utility Depreciation Practices, compiled by Depreciation Subcommittee of the National Association of Regulatory Utility Commissioners, 1968, NARUC, Washington, D.C.

Valuing a Business, Shannon P. Pratt, 1981, Dow Jones-Irwin, Homewood, Illinois.

Valuing Small Business and Professional Practices, Shannon P. Pratt, 1986, Dow Jones-Irwin, Homewood, Illinois.

The Appraisal of Real Estate, 1978, American Institute of Real Estate Appraisers, Chicago, Illinois.

FINANCIAL INFORMATION AND ANALYSIS

Various publications, Moody's Investors Service, Inc., New York.

Various publications, by subscription from Standard & Poor's Corporation, New York.

Investments—Analysis and Management, Jack Clark Francis, 1972, Mc-Graw-Hill, Inc., New York.

Investments, William F. Sharpe, 1981, Prentice-Hall, Inc., Englewood Cliffs, NJ.

Investment Analysis and Management, Anthony J. Curley and Robert M. Bear, 1979, Harper & Row Publishers, Inc., New York.

Various publications, by subscription, Value Line, Inc., New York.

"Blue Chip Economic Indicators", by subscription from Capital Publications, Inc., Alexandria, VA.

"I/B/E/S" Institutional Brokers Estimate System, Lynch, Jones & Ryan, New York.

"RMA Annual Statement Studies", published annually by Robert Morris Associates, Philadelphia, PA.

"Almanac of Business and Industrial Financial Ratios", Leo Troy, published annually by Prentice-Hall, Inc., Englewood Cliffs, NJ.

Mergerstat Review, published annually by W.T. Grimm & Co., Chicago, Illinois.

"Federal Reserve Bulletin", published monthly by the Board of Governors of the Federal Reserve System, Washington, D.C.

"Stocks, Bonds, Bills, and Inflation: Quarterly Service", published quarterly by Ibbotson Associates, Inc., Chicago, Illinois.

ACCOUNTING, TAXES

Purchase and Sale of Small Businesses, Marc J. Lane, 1985, John Wiley & Sons, New York.

Handbook of Modern Finance, ed. Dennis E. Logue, 1984, Warren, Gorham & Lamont, Boston, MA.

"Tax Management" Portfolios, by subscription from Tax Management Inc., division of The Bureau of National Affairs, Inc., Washington, D.C.

INTANGIBLE ASSETS

Taxation of Intellectual Property, Marvin Petry, 1986, Mathew Bender & Company, New York.

Patent and Trademark Tactics and Practice, David A. Burge, 1984, John Wiley & Sons, New York.

Trademarks, U.S. Department of Commerce, 1970, U.S. Government Printing Office, Washington, D.C.

INDEX